Social bliss considered: in marriage and divorce; cohabiting unmarried, and public whoring. ... With the speech of Miss Polly Baker; and notes thereon. By Gideon Archer.

Peter Annet

ECCO
PRINT EDITIONS

Eighteenth Century
Collections Online
Print Editions

Gale ECCO Print Editions

Relive history with *Eighteenth Century Collections Online*, now available in print for the independent historian and collector. This series includes the most significant English-language and foreign-language works printed in Great Britain during the eighteenth century, and is organized in seven different subject areas including literature and language; medicine, science, and technology; and religion and philosophy. The collection also includes thousands of important works from the Americas.

The eighteenth century has been called "The Age of Enlightenment." It was a period of rapid advance in print culture and publishing, in world exploration, and in the rapid growth of science and technology – all of which had a profound impact on the political and cultural landscape. At the end of the century the American Revolution, French Revolution and Industrial Revolution, perhaps three of the most significant events in modern history, set in motion developments that eventually dominated world political, economic, and social life.

In a groundbreaking effort, Gale initiated a revolution of its own: digitization of epic proportions to preserve these invaluable works in the largest online archive of its kind. Contributions from major world libraries constitute over 175,000 original printed works. Scanned images of the actual pages, rather than transcriptions, recreate the works *as they first appeared.*

Now for the first time, these high-quality digital scans of original works are available via print-on-demand, making them readily accessible to libraries, students, independent scholars, and readers of all ages.

For our initial release we have created seven robust collections to form one the world's most comprehensive catalogs of 18th century works.

Initial Gale ECCO Print Editions collections include:

History and Geography
Rich in titles on English life and social history, this collection spans the world as it was known to eighteenth-century historians and explorers. Titles include a wealth of travel accounts and diaries, histories of nations from throughout the world, and maps and charts of a world that was still being discovered. Students of the War of American Independence will find fascinating accounts from the British side of conflict.

Social Science
Delve into what it was like to live during the eighteenth century by reading the first-hand accounts of everyday people, including city dwellers and farmers, businessmen and bankers, artisans and merchants, artists and their patrons, politicians and their constituents. Original texts make the American, French, and Industrial revolutions vividly contemporary.

Medicine, Science and Technology
Medical theory and practice of the 1700s developed rapidly, as is evidenced by the extensive collection, which includes descriptions of diseases, their conditions, and treatments. Books on science and technology, agriculture, military technology, natural philosophy, even cookbooks, are all contained here.

Literature and Language
Western literary study flows out of eighteenth-century works by Alexander Pope, Daniel Defoe, Henry Fielding, Frances Burney, Denis Diderot, Johann Gottfried Herder, Johann Wolfgang von Goethe, and others. Experience the birth of the modern novel, or compare the development of language using dictionaries and grammar discourses.

Religion and Philosophy
The Age of Enlightenment profoundly enriched religious and philosophical understanding and continues to influence present-day thinking. Works collected here include masterpieces by David Hume, Immanuel Kant, and Jean-Jacques Rousseau, as well as religious sermons and moral debates on the issues of the day, such as the slave trade. The Age of Reason saw conflict between Protestantism and Catholicism transformed into one between faith and logic -- a debate that continues in the twenty-first century.

Law and Reference
This collection reveals the history of English common law and Empire law in a vastly changing world of British expansion. Dominating the legal field is the *Commentaries of the Law of England* by Sir William Blackstone, which first appeared in 1765. Reference works such as almanacs and catalogues continue to educate us by revealing the day-to-day workings of society.

Fine Arts
The eighteenth-century fascination with Greek and Roman antiquity followed the systematic excavation of the ruins at Pompeii and Herculaneum in southern Italy; and after 1750 a neoclassical style dominated all artistic fields. The titles here trace developments in mostly English-language works on painting, sculpture, architecture, music, theater, and other disciplines. Instructional works on musical instruments, catalogs of art objects, comic operas, and more are also included.

The BiblioLife Network

This project was made possible in part by the BiblioLife Network (BLN), a project aimed at addressing some of the huge challenges facing book preservationists around the world. The BLN includes libraries, library networks, archives, subject matter experts, online communities and library service providers. We believe every book ever published should be available as a high-quality print reproduction; printed on-demand anywhere in the world. This insures the ongoing accessibility of the content and helps generate sustainable revenue for the libraries and organizations that work to preserve these important materials.

The following book is in the "public domain" and represents an authentic reproduction of the text as printed by the original publisher. While we have attempted to accurately maintain the integrity of the original work, there are sometimes problems with the original work or the micro-film from which the books were digitized. This can result in minor errors in reproduction. Possible imperfections include missing and blurred pages, poor pictures, markings and other reproduction issues beyond our control. Because this work is culturally important, we have made it available as part of our commitment to protecting, preserving, and promoting the world's literature.

GUIDE TO FOLD-OUTS MAPS and OVERSIZED IMAGES

The book you are reading was digitized from microfilm captured over the past thirty to forty years. Years after the creation of the original microfilm, the book was converted to digital files and made available in an online database.

In an online database, page images do not need to conform to the size restrictions found in a printed book. When converting these images back into a printed bound book, the page sizes are standardized in ways that maintain the detail of the original. For large images, such as fold-out maps, the original page image is split into two or more pages

Guidelines used to determine how to split the page image follows:

• Some images are split vertically; large images require vertical and horizontal splits.
• For horizontal splits, the content is split left to right.
• For vertical splits, the content is split from top to bottom.
• For both vertical and horizontal splits, the image is processed from top left to bottom right.

SOCIAL BLISS

CONSIDERED:

In MARRIAGE and DIVORCE;
COHABITING UNMARRIED, and
PUBLIC WHORING.

CONTAINING

Things neceſſary to be known by all that ſeek
mutual Felicity, and are ripe for the Enjoyment of it.

WITH

The SPEECH of Miſs POLLY BAKER; and
Notes thereon.

————Man when created,
At firſt alone, long wandered up and down,
Forlorn and ſilent as his Vaſſal Beaſt;
But when a Heav'n-born Maid to him appear'd,
Strange Paſſion fill'd his Eyes, and fir'd his Heart,
Unloos'd his Tongue, and his firſt Talk was Love.

OTWAY.

By GIDEON ARCHER.
[Peter Annet]

LONDON:
Printed for and ſold by R. ROSE, near St. *Paul's*.
M. DCC. XLIX.

{ Price Two Shillings. }

THE
PREFACE.

THOSE that are worthy to know, and enjoy the rights of human nature, and the righteous liberties of mankind, will make a right use of them : To those it is given to understand and believe truths hid from them, whom reason cannot set free from the fetters of a false faith.

There are men of such unnatural gloomy sects, who believe, that God and nature take different sides, that piety consists in the mortification of natural appetites in practice, and the dictates of reason in matters of belief, that maintain an everlasting war with themselves and rebellion against nature, *to mortify the flesh with its affections and lusts;* hence reasonable pleasure is condemn'd and prohibited; tho' God has given these natural affections and lusts to be gratified with reason, to make life sweet and agreeable, that man may be better able to bear the bitter and sour that is in it, to keep his mind chearful from gloominess and despondency, and render his disposition chearful and easy. For the sake of rest, man endures labour, and for the pleasures of love, the fatigue and disquietudes of bringing up a family. Since we are thrown into life, and must accept of it so long as we are in it, *for better for worse;* let us enjoy the *better,* as well as the *worse,* as much as our nature and circumstances with reason will permit, or else the *yoke* of life will not be very *easy, nor the burden light.* If

A 2

we

we have not a moderate fhare of the good, as well as of the evil in life, 'tis not worth our having.

If God is offended with things that do, or do not offend man, and cannot affect him, he muft be the moft unhappy of all beings. We can therefore be only *faid* to offend God, when we break his laws; and laws contrary to our nature, our reafon and fitnefs of things for our benefit and fatisfaction in general, are not thofe laws that he has given us for our conduct?

Yet fuch a moody generation have many of the religious been, as to imagine, they pleafed God moft, when they moft difpleafed themfelves; but they that deny themfelves all the innocent gratifications of fenfe, what are they the better? Do they oblige or benefit God, or man, or themfelves, by their wayward actions?

Religion has been made to confift in a denial of thofe things moft, that pleafe the moft, to make it *fupernatural*; otherwife it is meer natural religion, but if we were fupernatural beings, it might be good reafoning Notwithftanding all thefe mighty pretenfions, the nature and pronenefs of men and women to embrace each other, is fo fitted and difpofed as God will have it, and gratifying the appetites and defires they have in common, tends to their common good, and notwithftanding what all men can fay, or do, nature is invincible and will be obey'd It is the judge or meafure *in* man, of what is good and evil *to* man.

Love and fociety, which are the greateft felicities in human life, unnatural religion endeavours to deftroy, by forbidding the mutual harmony of the different fex, and cloiftering them up feparate from fociety and the world; fo that fociety and the world receive no benefit from their being which they can withold; whereby *this* world is but

little

little in their debt, and 'twill be well for them if the *next* world be more in their debt.

What is more natural to young people than to defire to be married, and what can be more commendable and for the good of man, when it happens well? What worfe when it happens ill? Why then ought not marriage to be encouraged, and divorce allowed? Yet marriage is only permitted by St. *Paul* to prevent fornication; or rather he permits married perfons to enjoy one another for that reafon. 1 *Cor.* vii. 1, 2. *It is good for a man not to touch a woman; neverthelefs, to avoid fornication, let every man have his own wife, and every woman have her own hufband.* And ver. 5. *Defraud not one another, except it be with confent for a time, that you may give your felves to fafting and to prayer, and come together again, that Satan tempt you not for your incontinency.* Were it not for Satan's temptations, the defrauding one another would be no fraud: 'Tis the fear of him that makes faints honeft. That he recommends celibacy rather than matrimony, I think cannot be denied. *Ver.* 7, 8, 9. *I would that all men were even as I myfelf; but every one hath his proper gift of God, one after this manner and another after that. I fay therefore to the unmarried and widows, it is good for them if they abide even as I; but if they cannot contain, let them marry; for it is better to marry than to burn.* So, ver. 38 *He that giveth his virgin in marriage, doth well, but he that giveth her not, doth better.* You evidently fee celibacy is preferred to matrimony. And *ver* 39, 40 *The wife is bound by the law as long as the hufband liveth; but if her hufband be dead, fhe is at liberty to be married to whom fhe will, only in the Lord. But fhe is happier, if fhe fo abide after my judgment, and I think alfo I have the fpirit of God.* 1 *Tim.* v. 11. *The younger wi-*

dows

dows refuse, for when they have begun to wax wan-
ton against Chrift *they will marry, having damna-*
tion, because they caft off their firft faith. So that
according to the doctrine of St. *Paul,* when people are ripened to the fenfe of feeling, and find
the glowing warmth of all infpiring nature kird-
ling them to love and procreation, it is notwithftanding *good,* if they can poffibly forbear, *not to touch*
each other A doctrine deftructive of mutual happinefs, and if it could be practifed by all, would depo-
pulate mankind, and finifh human race. Why then
were the different fex made ? Why is copulation
finful only in man ? Why have they fuch ftrong
propenfities to it, that they run all hazards for the
fake of enjoyment ? Why have they when mature
and in the moft perfect ftate of health, fuch impulfe
to it, as is next to invincible ? If the action be evil,
why was there not another way found out of pro-
ducing the human fpecies ? If it be proper to
thank God for our exiftence, is it proper to blame
the means or inftruments he makes ufe of to ac-
complifh the end, for which we give thanks.
If it be evil to give pain to, or take away
life from any of the human kind ; is not the
contrary a good, *v.z.* to give pleafure, produce
life, and maintain the production. A nature and
confequence oppofite to evil muft be good ; for oppofite natures cannot both be evil, unlefs they are
extremes, and the good corfifts in a medium, but
in the prefent cafe, a medium is indolence, and
confifts in doing neither, or nothing. If therefore
one be condemnable, the other fhould be commendable. But tho' unmarried people's begetting
and bringing up children, is not a laudable action
by our laws ; yet is not the charge and trouble
which is the confequence of the action, punifhment
enough ? If fuch do no injury to themfelves, they
do

do none to the public. 'Tis not good to bring children into being, without taking care of that being: For creatures had better never be, than be miferable. Therefore to beget children in wedlock, and not to provide for them, cannot be good; to produce and provide for them, tho' not in wedlock, cannot be evil. What then is it fanctifies one more than the other, when both are equally good to their offspring, but human law? To be the means of giving exiftence, is with re-fpect to man a thing of chance; therefore what good attends it, is in parents taking care of their offspring, by educating them according to their ability: What duty is due from children to their parents is for this, not for their exiftence. To beget a child is neither a good nor evil action in it-felf, the means or meer action is barely following the impulfe of nature; but the good or evil of it is according to the circumftances attending it. Life in itfelf is neither good nor evil; the good that is in being, is in well-being; and the evil of it, lies in being miferable. Marriage does not make the begetters of children parents more than nature does, they that are propeily fo, difcharge their part to their offspring, and deferve no blame. Doctrines that prevent marriage as much as poffible, and when they cannot prevent, make it miferable, by refufing redrefs to the unhappy, are doctrines of fuch piety as confift in rebellion againft nature, which muft have very pernicious effects: For nature will be obeyed, and ought to be fo under the conduct of reafon.

I own myfelf pretty much indebted to that fub-lime reafoner as well as poet, Mr. JOHN MILTON, on the fubject of divorce: And the quotations which have no author, are his, to which my own experience of happy and unhappy wedlock

hath

hath been no fmall incitement. The following feeling arguments flow from one that has had a two-fold experience in matrimonial bonds of blifs and mifery, love and envy. honour and contempt in ftates as contrary as light and darknefs, and as wide as heaven and hell, that have been like the years of plenty and famine in *Egypt* ; fo that the former plenty was forgotten by the following famine, or like the rich man in torment with a retrofpection of paft felicity never more to return ; the once joyous days of affection and felicity, eclips'd by a fullen conftellation of malignant influence, bringing confufion within doors and without. Let filence conceal the reft. *Tell it not in* Gath, *publifh it not in* Afkelon, *left the daughters of* rebellion *rejoice, and the daughters of* wantonnefs and ingratitude *triumph.*

SOCIAL BLISS

CONSIDER'D.

THE words to which we are referred by *Jesus Christ*, as the original institution of marriage, are in *Genesis* ii. where the Lord God is represented as having first made *Adam* to live by himself like a batchelor, perhaps that he might know the difference between that and a married state, and how the addition of a social mate heightened his bliss. Whether it be true or not, as a history, it administers a very delicate fable, or parable; for from thence most excellent lessons for matrimonial comfort and instruction may be collected.

The passage affords proper subject for meditation, to all those that are already entered, or would enter into matrimonial engagements: And this is sufficient for my present purpose.

In *Genesis* ii. 18, &c. it is given us thus: *And the Lord God said, it is not good that man should be alone, I will make an help meet for him.*

Ver. 21. *And the Lord God caused a deep sleep to fall upon* Adam, *and he slept; and he took one of his ribs, and closed up the flesh instead thereof.*

B   22.

22. *And the rib which the Lord God had taken from man made he a woman, and brought her unto the man.*

23. *And Adam said, this is now bone of my bones, and flesh of my flesh: She shall be called woman, because she was taken out of man.*

24. *Therefore shall a man leave his father and his mother, and shall cleave unto his wife: And they shall be one flesh.*

25. *And they were both naked, the man and his wife, and were not ashamed.*

I have selected this passage for my meditation, not as a natural history, but as a divine fable; the moral of which, I intend to shew, is fraught with the most useful lessons for matrimonial happiness.

It is well known that the wisdom of the Ancients was delivered in allegories, and the wise only understood their meaning. This was done, perhaps, to inform men that the fountain of wisdom conceals itself under the veil of created objects, that constantly presenting themselves to their bodily senses pass and repass before them, and are not reflected on with any depth of thought but by men of penetration and insight; these only *see the Lord in his sanctuary:* That is, *God in his creatures.* Any other manner of seeing God we seek in vain, for a different or distinct vision of him from this, *no man ever did or can see.* It is adhering so strictly, and contending so zealously, for what men know nothing of, *viz.* the truth of the letter in all its parts, which makes people formally religious, and no more; and by this means they lose what they contend for, *religion* itself, or the true spirit, life and essence of it. And by reason of the intricacy and unusefulness of the argument to answer this plain and useful end, in going about to convince biblical Infidels

of

of the veracity of the letter which they call
facred, they make many more Infidels, and confirm thofe that are * ; becaufe the reafonings and
circumftances that appear in this age, can in no
wife illuftrate or corroborate things of a different
kind; of which, no tract of proof remains in the prefent ftate of things ; and men of no vulgar infpec-
tion will not be deluded by diftant profpects and
reprefentations, which being differently and clofe-
ly perceived by their natural light, muft neceffarily appear to them as fictitious, with fig-leaf
coverings. I fhall therefore take another courfe,
not to perfuade difbelievers out of their fenfes, or
differently than their common fenfe perfuades
them and prevails with them to conceive ; but to
employ their conceptions aright in an ufeful and
proper manner, without their being over-awed by
authority, or deluded by enthufiafm, from making a true judgment of things, and drawing
therefrom rational and ufeful deductions.

We are not to fuppofe by the paffage of this
antique Scripture before cited, becaufe the God
is reprefented faying, *It is not good for man
to be alone*, that the making of woman was an
after-thought in God, when he had tried how man
would be in a lonely ftate, as might be fuggefted
from the hiftory ; this is a thought unbecoming
us of Deity : But that divine wifdom gives the
preference of human happinefs to a matrimonial
ftate, and has given woman for the folace and

B 2   delight

---

* As the Apoftle fays of others , *In going about to eftablifh
their own righteoufnifs, they have not fubmitted to the righteoufnefs of God.* Where's the neceffity of making the belief of
human hiftory a part of religion, if men may be made virtuous and pious without fuch belief ? Is it not contending more
for the covering, than the body ; and neglecting *the one thing
needful?* Nay, it is defpifing or neglecting a pearl, for a barley-
corn , and, by contending for the fhadow, like *Æfop's* dog in
the fable, the fubftance is loft.

delight of man. She is to be a remedy againſt lonelineſs, to be chearful and gay, to comfort and delight him. This ſhews us, that the end and deſign of matrimony is to add to man's felicity ; therefore, when this end proves abortive, the means are of no value ; and that matrimony which docs not add to man's happineſs, is not of a divine inſtitution : There is nothing ſacred nor moral, nor any good policy in it. A moral inſtitution not effecting a moral end, is of no moral validity ; and therefore ought to be rectified to make it effective, or be eſteemed (as it is) of no force or conſequence.

It is not good that man ſhould be alone ; therefore it was not the deſign of divine wiſdom that man ſhould live a lonely life, without the friendly and comfortable aid of female help: Therefore ſaid God, *I will make a help meet*, or fit *for him* This ſhews us what a true wife is, or what a wife ought to be, a *help* fit for the man ſhe has · She muſt be a help, and a proper help, or ſhe is no wife, tho' ſhe may bear the name ; and if ſhe is no wife, the man is not married, he is not in the ſtate of matrimony, it is in the nature of the thing, and ought to be in fact declared null and void; and conſequently ſuch a man has a right to ſeek him a wife, one that is a help proper for him, for the former bands are broke, the covenant is void, becauſe the conditions are not performed · For *it is not good that men ſhould be alone*, and ſeeing he finds his wants as great as before, and his lonelineſs in formal matrimony not cured in one, he has a right to ſeek his own good in another, by diſſolving that which nature had before diſſolved, for that is by this declared invalid, and to have loſt its force having not the intrinſic goodneſs it ought to have. And *it is not good that man ſhould be alone*, but

have

have *a help meet for him*: He that hath not a proper help in a female is alone, or in a lonely uncomfortable ftate, which it is not good for him to be in.

God made woman for man, and gave her to him, to be the folace and comfort of his life: She therefore that is an affiftant, a fit and proper aid and comforter to a man, is a wife. I think it requires fome peculiar explanation to make thefe words of God, *viz It is not good for man to be alone,* and thofe of St. *Paul* to harmonize, *It is good for a man not to touch a woman.* But of this, and why men generally find mifery in a matrimonial ftate defign'd by nature for their happinefs, and what is the remedy, I intend in the fequel to fhew.

And the Lord God caufed a deep fleep to fall upon Adam, *and he flept.* The production of woman was not intended to give man pain, but to obtund his pains with growing pleafure. *And he flept:* Man being on the brink of matrimony becomes contemplative, he is thrown into a mufing ftate. *And he took one of his ribs:* All nature is then at work within him *And he clofed up the flefh inftead thereof:* Love foftens the nature of man. *And the rib which the Lord God had taken from man made he a woman:* The nature of man and woman is as nearly the fame, as a man's *rib* is to his body. This in general, but more particularly, this was to make *Adam* a wife. A man's wife therefore, is to be confidered as a part of his own body; but this cannot be in a natural and moral fenfe, unlefs one nature and confederate moral conduct be in both; if both love alike, both will agree to act alike. The heart is defended with the ribs, a wife indeed is the defender and preferver of her hufband's heart, not only by engroffing his whole heart, and guarding
the

the avenues of his love and life, but by her softnefs and pliablenefs; healing every wound, or relieving every pain that affects his heart, *He clofed up the flefh in room thereof.* Her foft endearing nature clofes up every breach, heals the moft dangerous difcord, and mollifies the moft pungent affliction. *And brought her to the man:* This double-refin'd human nature, this charming form of complaifancy and delight, the finifh'd piece of this orb of creatures, replete with every fhining grace and neceffary virtue yet wanting in man to fill up the meafure of his happinefs, was given to woman; and woman for this end was given to man. Nature could go no higher, could produce no greater work, nor man could more defire.

And Adam *faid, This is bone of my bones, and flefh of my flefh; fhe fhall be called woman, becaufe fhe was taken out of man.* Adam knew her original, by her form and nature, fo like himfelf; and confequently her behaviour was fo pleafing, that he pronounced her to be his own. This appears to be all the fimple form of ceremony, by which they were united. We do not read, that God acted the part of a prieft to join them together, only that of a father to the young woman, in giving her away. *For he brought her to the man:* Therefore the father's confent with the damfel, I conceive to be ceremony fufficient to confecrate matrimony. If a man thus take a woman, and declares her before God, or before good witnefs, to be his wife, is all I can find in the original inftitution. But the prefent circumftances of things generally make fome particular conditions or covenants neceffary.

A woman who is a meet help to a man, the comfort and folace of his life, that is, *as bone*

of

of his bones, and flesh of his flesh; or, as if she was taken out of him, that is as dear to him as his own flesh and blood and bones, is a joining worthy of God: From such a wife a man would as soon break one of his bones as be divorced. One flesh and bone is one body, and one body will have one soul; her existence must seem to be from him, and his life to be bound up in her.

Therefore shall a man leave his father and mother, and shall cleave unto his wife, and they shall be one flesh. Such as are so united, are of God's joining. To such a wife as has been described, a man becomes nearer related in soul or affection than to his father or mother, from whom his body and soul descended. By the time children come to a state of maturity, the affection between them and their parents is much lessened; then a new affection is raised and increased towards a wife, with whom, when there is an union in spirit, it is a joining, fit to be ascribed to him who is a Spirit There can be no nearer relation, than such who are so joined. He that before was one flesh of his parents, is now become one flesh with his wife, as if all that is dear now centered in her, they are one flesh in likeness of nature, in fitness of mind, and disposition. The same flesh must have the same spirit; the same soul must be in both, they cannot otherwise be united as one flesh. " As the " unity of minds is greater than that of bodies, " so the dissimilitude is greater, the difference " and distinction more unlike. The likeness or " unlikeness in human nature joins or disjoins " the human kind irresistibly A man cannot " leave father and mother and cleave to a no- " thing, to a worse than nothing, to an adversary. " Can any law be so unreasonable or inhuman to

" make

" make men cleave to calamity, to mifery, to
" Ruin!" When the parties joining are only of
man's joining, that is, without the effential property
of a cementing nature; as is too generally the cafe,
when the regard is had to mammon, or to gender only, what is it better than covetoufnefs or
whoredom?

I come now to confider the laft verfe of the
paffage before cited, which fays, *And they were
both naked, the man and his wife, and were not
afhamed.* The needleffnefs of this expreffion
fhews fome deeper fenfe is aim'd at in this matter
than what is barely narrative; what need had the
writer, as an hiftorian, to add thefe words; for
this muft be neceffarily underftood, and known
by every reader, they were hufband and wife,
Mr. *Adam* and Mrs. *Adam* *, and there was neither man nor woman to fee them naked as they
were; of what then fhould they be afhamed?
But the myftical, fpiritual and internal fenfe is,
that they were both innocent before God, and
knew no evil in their enjoyments, therefore were
not confcious of guilt. *Adam* was rouz'd to
fruition at the great call of Nature, and *Eve*
fpontaneoufly acquiefc'd without offence. In this
they obeyed the command of the Lord God, *Increafe and multiply:* Thus they anfwered the end
of their maker's will, and finned not.

The ceremonies of marriage are various, a-
mong various nations and people; but whatever
they are, they are but ceremonies, which law
and cuftom only make neceffary, and are the
leaft part of matrimony, therefore thofe that act
towards each other on the principles of natural
honefty, without any tie but that of confcience
and

* *Genefis* v 2 *Male and Female created he them, and bleffed
them, and called their name* Adam, *in the day when they were
created.*

and conftant affection, tho' they fin indeed against the cuftom of the country, yet not to God, before whom *they walk naked and are not afhamed.* And tho' men may endeavour to put thofe to fhame that tranfgrefs the laws of men, yet the generality of thofe that fubmit to human impofitions, inconfiftent with the reafon and nature of the matrimonial ftate, are forced to own in the fecret fenfe and forrow of their fouls, if not in words, that *it is a yoke, which neither they nor their fathers were ever able to bear*, that is to fay, fuch is the ill-coupling of unfit perfons, who are neither pair'd in bodies, nor match'd in minds, it is moft barbarous confining them in a ftate worfe than *Algerine* flavery during life. All that I intend to plead for, is a reafonable liberty of obeying the righteous laws of God and nature, that are confiftent with human happinefs, the great end defign'd in a matrimonial ftate : And whatever cuftoms do by their natural confequence fruftrate that end, do alfo make void the inftitution, which originally aiming at the happinefs of the contracting parties is fubverted, and confequently annulled, when, by vicious law or cuftom, it generally and naturally tends to their unhappinefs But I intend not hereby to excite any to evil practice, but to fet in a clear light what virtuous freedom ought to be enjoyed, and what natural liberty may be indulged, confiftent with private happinefs and the publick tranquility. Virtuous actions do not arife from conftraint, but from natural inftinct, pure motives, and human affections.

I have confidered the original inftitution of matrimony, or what is recommended to us for fuch ; and have found the true nature of it in the qualifications of a wife, from what is given us as the

C

history

history of the *first Adam*, the supposed father of mankind: I intend next to consider, what (as we are told) the *second Adam* (as he is call'd) has said on this subject.

The words I intend to consider, are in *Matthew* xix. ỹ 3. to the 12th.

3 *The Pharisees also came unto him, and saying unto him, Is it lawful for a man to put away his wife for every cause?*

4. *And he answered and said unto them, have ye not read, that he which made them at the beginning made them male and female?*

5. *And said, for this cause shall a man leave father and mother, and shall cleave to his wife; and they twain shall be one flesh.*

6. *Wherefore they are no more twain, but one flesh; what therefore God hath joined together let not man put asunder.*

7. *They say unto him, why did* Moses *then command to give a writing of divorcement, and put her away?*

8 *He saith unto them,* Moses, *because of the hardness of your hearts, suffered you to put away your wives; but from the beginning it was not so.*

9. *And I say unto you, whosoever shall put away his wife, except it be for fornication, and shall marry another, committeth adultery, and whoso marrieth her, which is put away, doth commit adultery.*

10 *His disciples say unto him, if the case of a man be so with his wife, it is not good to marry.*

11 *But he said unto them, all men cannot receive this saying, save they to whom it is given.*

12. *For there are some eunuchs, which were so born from their mother's womb, and there are some eunuchs which are made eunuchs of men;*

and

and there be eunuchs which have made themselves eunuchs, for the kingdom of heaven's sake. He that is able to receive it, let him receive it.

St. *Mark*, chap x relates it thus :

Ver. 2. *And the Pharisees come to him, and asked him, is it lawful for a man to put away his wife? tempting him*

3 *And he answered and said unto them, what did* Moses *command you ?*

4. *And they said,* Moses *suffered to write a bill of divorcement, and to put her away*

5 *And* Jesus *answered and said unto them, for the hardness of your heart he wrote you this precept.*

6. *But from the beginning of the creation God made them male and female*

7. *For this cause shall a man leave his father and mother, and cleave to his wife.*

8 *And they twain shall be one flesh ; so then they are no more twain, but one flesh.*

9. *What therefore God hath joined together, let not man put asunder*

10 *And in the house the disciples asked him again of the same matter.*

11. *And he saith unto them, whosoever shall put away his wife, and marry another, committeth adultery against her*

12 *And if a woman shall put away her husband, and be married to another, she committeth adultery.*

It is evident, that these two relations of the same fact do not exactly agree. The question put by the Pharisees, is not the same in one as in another, nor *Christ's* answer to them the same ; nor do the words cited, agree with those they refer to , therefore, whatever error may be found in them, said to be spoken by *Jesus Christ*, is not to

be

be attributed to him, but to the writers: For the difagreement of a relation fhews the imperfection of the relaters; and that they had not a critical regard to truth or knowledge of it, as its profeffed promulgators ought to have. But thefe, tho' faints, were men, and, as men, were liable to err: Therefore they (or fome others in their name, which is ftill more likely) might poffibly deliver to us, as the words of *Chrift*, fuch words as were never fpoken by him. This I am neceffitated to acknowledge, to clear our Lord of fpeaking fuch words *as never man fpake* that were fpake becoming a man, which are afcribed in fome of the foregoing words to him, and which are *not true*, compar'd with the original referr'd to, nor right in the nature of things

It may be thought by fome, that the errors here complained of, are fmall, and therefore ought to have been foftly paffed over, or that, however, it does not deferve fo fevere a cenfure. I would willingly make the beft of it, even by fpiritualizing the letter away, if the cafe would allow it; but this difcourfe of *Jefus Chrift* and the Pharifees is not of that nature to bear fuch ufage, without committing violence to the text; and the text is of fuch fort, as will upon examination appear to be given by the fpirit of the church, a fpirit, that under a pretence of extraordinary refin'd fanctity, is deftructive of human happinefs and human exiftence; and therefore I cannot fuppofe *Jefus Chrift* the author of this difcourfe, which in *Matthew* and *Mark* is afcribed to him.

The queftion afked *Jefus Chrift* by the Pharifees in *Matthew* and *Mark*, is not the fame. In the *former* it is, *Is it Lawful for a man to put away his wife, for* EVERY *caufe?* In the *latter*, the queftion feems to be, Whether a man may put away his wife for ANY caufe? As there is a vaft

difference

difference between thefe queftions, fo they require a different anfwer; the former a negative,
the latter a pofitive one; becaufe it is not fit to indulge a capricious humour with too arbitrary a
power; but a reafonable authority to punifh in-
corrigible offenders, is neceffary in every fort of
government: And as it is not fit a man fhould
gratify a peevifh temper for every flight occafion,
fo it is not fit he fhould be obliged to bear all a-
bufes, infults and conftant provocations from an
implacable fpirit, without ability to remedy his
condition. Nor is it more tolerable on the woman's fide, that has the misfortune to be daily
abufed by an unnatural brute, falfely called a
hufband.

St *Mark* fays, the Pharifees afked *Jefus* this
queftion, *tempting him*. I fuppofe, he means, to
try or know his judgment, he being, as 'tis faid or
fuppofed, of the fect of the *Effenes*, who profeffed
a community of goods, and fhunn'd all pleafures,
even marriage, and all carnal copulation with
women; from whence, perhaps, the chriftian
monkery took its rife. I muft own, it is *tempting* the reader to know what St. *Mark* means by
the words *tempting him*.

And, faith Matthew, *he anfwered and faid unto
them, have ye not read, that he which made them at
the beginning, made them male and female; and
faid, for this caufe fhall a man leave father and
mother, and fhall cleave to his wife, and they
twain fhall be one flefh?* Had I been one of the
Pharifees, I fhould have replied, No certainly, we
have not read any fuch thing, that he who made
man at the beginning faid thefe words, for where
we have thefe words in *Genefis*, (which have been
already confidered) they either appear to be the
words of *Adam*, or of the writer, not of *Adam*'s
maker. It's plain, the writers of the New Tefta-
ment

ment were not well acquainted with the Old, by most things they cite from thence. This citation is false, and falsly applied; therefore these are not the words of the *Lord Jesus, who knew all things,* but of the ignorant writers, who knew not what they were writing about, and refer to a history that they did not understand.

Now, if the foundation which the argument is built on is wrong, then the argument is false, and the consequence drawn from it erroneous. Here it says, *because God made man male and female, therefore man shall leave his father and mother, and cleave to his wife.* In *Genesis* it says no such thing: There we read, that *Adam* said, *This is now bone of my bones, and flesh of my flesh, she shall be called woman, because she was taken out of man. Therefore shall a man leave father and mother, and cleave unto his wife, and they shall be one flesh.* 'Tis not clear, whether the latter verse contains the words of *Adam,* or of the historian, but 'tis very clear they are not the words of *Adam*'s Maker. In *Matthew* and *Mark,* 'tis said, *God created man male and female, and for this cause shall a man leave his father and mother and cleave to his wife* Is the difference of gender then all that is necessary for matrimony? And is it for *this* cause that God has joined them together, and no man must put them asunder? Are we admonish'd not to marry, merely for the gratification of carnal lust; and is this, notwithstanding, represented to be the sole cause why a man should leave father and mother, and cleave to his wife? Why may he not, for the same reason, cleave to a harlot? If this be a sufficient qualification for God's joining, these also are joined together by him: For St *Paul* says, *he that is joined to a harlot is one flesh.* Therefore God's creating them male and female is not the true and

sole

fole caufe that conftitutes man and wife ; therefore the meer joining male to female is not what
is meant by God's joining, and therefore we are
mifinform'd when we are told, that *he who made
them in the beginning, made them male and female,
and faid* FOR THIS CAUSE *fhall a man leave father and mother, and cleave to his wife* Nor does
the formality of joining, call'd the ordinance,
make it of God's joining ; for is all that the par-
fon does, God's doings? If ever it was efteemed
fo, it muft have been when parfons were efteemed
as Gods : None but idolaters efteem them fo now.
If the ceremony that joins them, makes it God's
joining, tho' done by man, let it be proved that
it was ordered and prefcribed of God in any other
fenfe than what human laws and ceremonies
may be faid to be ; or that God's joining can be
underftood in any other light than the moral of
the fable in *Genefis* directs us to, which has been
explained, *viz. It is not good that man fhould be
alone, I will make an help meet for him.* But the
words contain no prohibition, that man may not
put afunder what man puts together.

Yet what is moft furprifing, *Jefus Chrift* (as his
words are fet forth to us) fo far difcountenances
the joining of male and female, as if he intended to abolifh his father's law, *increafe and multiply*, as well as the law of *Mofes*, for divorce:
For, to prevent marriage and multiplication, he
is faid to recommend celibacy and mutilation ;
too plainly, I fear, to be denied, and too grofly
to be defended, as will hereafter appear.

If the queftion of the Pharifees was, as in *matthew, Is it lawful for a man to put away his wife
for every caufe?* Then the anfwer given to it carries the matter from one extreme to another ; and
Jefus Chrift by interpreting the law of *Mofes* concerning divorce, condemns and annuls it, if the
answer

anfwer means that thofe joined by men, are of God's joining; for the following words are, *What therefore God has joined together let not man put afunder*; This interpreting the law of *Mofes* is, as we are obliged to interpret the gofpel, expound many of its precepts and doctrines away, to make th·m agree with reafon: But the anfwer of *Jefus Chrift* contains an explanation contrary to the reafon and fitnefs of the thing, if the fenfe of the text be as is commonly underftood. If it is to be otherwife taken, who can be certain he hits the truth in explaining a text, when the text itfelf appears to be fo far off from the truth, that in order to find the one, we are obliged to explain away the other.

'Tis no wonder the *Jews* believed *Jefus* not to be of God, becaufe they believed *Mofes* was, and that he had faithfully delivered to them the laws of God; if *Jefus* therefore fignified that God had given different laws to men, than *Mofes* gave; this ftrongly implied to them that were prepoffeffed in their opinions in favour of *Mofes*, that *Jefus* was not of God, becaufe he in contradiction to his own declaration that he *came not to deftroy the law, but to fulfil it*, deftroyed the law by explaining it away. And they might probably argue, that it was impoffible that God having an immutable will, (as muft be the confequence of perfect wifdom) fhould give different laws to his people at different times: And therefore perhaps, it is, that in the facred book the law or cuftom of facrifices is as old as *Cain* and *Abel*. On this confideration 'tis no wonder I fay, *they could not believe*, and that God himfelf had by this means *hardened their hearts*. What a meffage then was the Meffiah fent about!

The Pharifees objected their law of divorce given by *Mofes*, to thofe words, *what therefore God has*

has joined together, let not man put asunder. No
doubt but what God does is right, and we are not
to blame his doings ; but then the great diffi-
culty is to know what God's doings are, distinct
from man's in this case, if they are not to be understood in a *moral* sense. In this sense, who those
are that God joins together, we have seen in the
case of *Adam* and *Eve* referred to, and consequently what marriages are properly of God's joining ;
and that such persons who are as dear to each other
as their *own flesh and blood and bones*, as their *own
souls*, all men must own that no man ought to put
asunder. And this also implies, that such are not
so joined, who are not proper helps to each other,
but the contrary, tho' male and female : if such
come together, they are not husband and wife,
and therefore *ought to be put asunder.* Every
command given with reason binds our obedience
no otherwise than that reason holds, and a command *without* reason is arbitrary ; *against* reason,
is unjust ; both these bind no longer than the power
binds. But that all who are married by the priest,
are of God's joining, and therefore ought never to be
parted , or that their being *male* and *female* is all the
necessary qualification for that institution, cannot be
the meaning though it be the letter of the expression ;
and therefore if these were the words of *Christ*,
he spake a great deal more, which the transcribers
or priests have curtailed and mangled, to give it a
Jesuitical explanation for the service of the church,
the sons of which always make *him* say what serves
their turn, and to reason as weakly as they are
wicked.

If man, because they are *male* and *female*, are
to be joined together, this reason will ever take
place ; but this is *carnal* reason : Nor, if this be
all that joins them, *man* need not put them a-
D   sunder;

funder ; for they will come afunder of themfelves.

Becaufe of the hardnefs of your hearts, Mofes *wrote
you this precept* of divorce, which runs thus :
Deut. xxiv. 1. *When a man hath taken a wife, and
married her, and it come to pafs that fhe find no
favour in his eyes, becaufe he hath found fome uncleannefs in her ; then let him write her a bill of
divorcement, and give it in her hand, and fend
her out of his houfe.* The meaning of which, I
fuppofe to be, that when a woman, which a man
has taken to be his wife, is become a filthy creature in his eyes, and he cannot love her, let him
put her away ; for this is the only remedy to
make both parties eafy, fince a woman of any
good and tender difpofition muft be very unhappy to fee herfelf contemned and defpifed by
her hufband, and confequently much better pleafed
to be rid of fuch a hufband, and throw herfelf
into the arms of one that fhe can render herfelf
agreeable to, and will treat her with humanity.
and tendernefs. And a man the more he is con-
ftrained to live with a woman, that is difagreeable to him, will hate her the more. That the
hufband might not ufe this power capricioufly,
Mofes does not permit him to take her again :
Therefore wifely adds, *and when fhe is departed
out of his houfe, fhe may go and be another man's
wife. And if the latter hufband hate her, and
write her a bill of divorcement, and giveth it into
her hand, and fendeth her out of his houfe ; or if
the latter hufband die, which took her to be his wife,
her former hufband which fent her away may not
take her again to be his wife, after that fhe is de-
filed ; for that is an abomination before the Lord,*
&c. Now, if this permiffive law was given by
Mofes, fo were the reft ; for after this, and feveral
others that follow, *Chap.* xxvi. 16. *Mofes* tells them,
faying,

saying, *This day the Lord thy God hath commanded thee to do these statutes and judgments.* So that *Moses* had this law from God, as much as he had others; and therefore, whatever may be supposed or insinuated of one law, may be supposed or insinuated of all the rest.

'Tis hard to know or understand what this saying means. *Moses, because of the hardness of your heart, wrote you this precept* If this charges *Moses* with imposing bad laws on his nation, in the name of God, then he gave them laws to please them, rather than such as were good If God gave man a different law from the beginning than *Moses* afterwards gave, that law of *Moses* was different from the law of God; and there can be no better pretence for repealing it. But how this appears to be true, the Bible no where discovers *Adam* could not put away his wife, nor she him, and marry another, if there was not another man nor woman in the world, and it would be a great reflection on him that made *Adam*, that he could not, or would not make a woman to please him; but, on the contrary we are told, God made a *help meet for him*, and made her out of such stuff as *Adam* could not chuse but love, if he loved himself. Therefore this instance is not applicable to the case of divorce, nothing can justly be reasoned from it, and that which is, appears to be in the common sense of it, a sophistical and unintelligible expression, not well formed from the premises, nor applicable to the purpose There are scarce any precepts or principles, said to be delivered by *Jesus Christ*, that are not either distant from plainness, or from truth, if taken according to the strict letter sense, hence it is, that men learn and are never the better, and hence it is, that such instructions have done little good in the world; and that the teachers themselves

cannot

cannot agree, becaufe they cannot underftand.
Therefore, hitherto the fenfe of this boafted reve-
lation is unreveal'd ; and therefore hath not, becaufe it could not bring *peace on earth, and good
will to men* , but, on the contrary, *fire and fword,*
which was will'd* to be kindled by the revealer,
and ever fince has been, and is ever like to be,
the *everlafting fire that never can be quenched* So
true it is, that *without a parable fpake he not unto
them,* that what are delivered to us for his words
want fo much expounding, that one might be al-
moft tempted to think them delivered fo darkly,
as if on purpofe to oblige the expofitors and com-
mentators, and keep up the fpiritual traffick of
the myfteries of the kingdom, which create factions, fchifms and divifions. If you afk to what
end, or for what caufe then *Chrift* came, he is faid
himfelf to anfwer : *Suppofe ye that I come to give
peace on earth, I tell you nay, but rather divifion,*
&c. That this has been the confequence of his
coming, believers are forced to own . Why then
may we not believe him that he came for that purpofe, if the letter be true, fince himfelf confeffes
it ? But, fay Infidels, As fcarce any man that intends
mifchief, publickly declares it, this is as ftrong a
proof of enthufiafm as can be given ; and what from
another man, would fhock every reader. Can
any thing worfe, fay they, be faid of him, than he
here is reported to fay of himfelf ? I fay *reported,*
for I cannot believe *Jefus Chrift* faid thefe words ,
which is the only defence I can make, becaufe to
me they feem to be indefenfible For Infidels
further argue, that tho' this expreffion may, by
art and a lucky thought, be made to put on a fpiritual meaning, who can prove that the fpeaker's
meaning (or writer's rather) was the fame as the
expounder's, why then, fay they, muft it be wrapt
up

* *Luke* 49. 5.

up in the spirit, and expounded away? And if it be literally true, 'tis terrible! I must confess I cannot answer these objections, and therefore I put forth the riddle to them that assisted by the grace of *Christ* can do it, and whose business it is so to do, who are *ambassadors in Christ's stead*. I must own, that I think had *Christ* uttered such an expression, it had been wisdom to conceal it. Methinks it is pity he in his great humility chose *the fools of this world*, as he did, to be the historians of his life; for it must be matter of concern to believers, to read in so *holy* a book what cannot possibly be productive of any good, and gives the enemies of our blessed Lord and his holy Gospel occasion of reproach and triumph. This is an ill recommendation of the Gospel and character of *Jesus*. But these things should be treated tenderly, lest the profane have them in derision, and the enemy exulting say, as of pious *David* and his men of old, *Where is now their God?* or, as *Pilate* said of *Christ*, when crowned with thorns, *Behold the man*. It must be confessed, that the doctrines even of truth, delivered in obscure phrases, lead the mind from the path of truth, and raise up enemies against it.

The law that is against divorce, is against virtuous nature, because it hinders nature from taking its course, when virtue is the only motive that it should do so to promote a life of love and virtue, which a vicious mate is destructive of. What law soever prevents this, cannot be good, but is injurious to human felicity, and destructive of moral virtue, of religion and humanity. The author of such law cannot possibly be esteemed the redeemer, but must necessarily be judged to be the enslaver of mankind. To make *Christ* therefore the author of this law, is blaspheming his character as a redeemer, and degrading his divine dignity.

For

For as matrimony now is, " If we do but err in
" our choice (the moſt unblameable error that can
" be, being blind to future events) when the mighty
" conjoining ſyllables are pronounced by thoſe
" that take upon them to join heaven and hell
" together unpardonably till death pardons ; this
" that looked but now like a divine bleſſing with
" a graceful ſmile and gentle reaſon, ſtrait vaniſh-
" es like a fair ſky, and brings on ſuch a ſcene
" of clouds and tempeſt as turns all to ſhipwreck,
" without a haven or ſhore, but ranſomleſs cap-
" tivity " We are allowed to procure and apply
phyſical remedies againſt diſeaſes of the body, and
why not againſt diſeaſes of the mind, in, and ariſ-
ing from a matrimonial ſtate ? And why not a-
gainſt the ſtate of matrimony as the ſtate of the
public ? For that which is of private concern to
every one, is of public concern to all. Do not
grievances of the ſtate and the mind deſerve and
demand our regard and remedy, as much as thoſe
of the body ?

When marriage does not mend a man's ſtate,
it marrs it , if it does not cure his loneſomeneſs,
it makes him more lonely than a ſingle life, wherein a man naturally ſeeks the comfort his condition
affords, or ſeeks with hope to mend it In an uncomfortable married condition, the man or woman
beholds the perpetual ſcene of diſappointment always preſent, and perpetually feels ~~the ſenſe of~~ its
anguiſh, which diſpoſes the unhappy wretch to
loneſomeneſs, dejection ~~of mind~~ and melancholy,
to a diſagreeable ſtate of mind and dangerous conduct ; tho' male and female have been join'd ·
This then is not marriage, where the harmony of
ſouls is wanting

Theſe things being conſidered, the queſtion will
be, Whether *Moſes* gave the law of divorce to indulge *hardneſs of heart*, or whether it is not rather
hard-

hard heartednefs to deny the liberty of feparation to thofe who are miferably joined ? Is this *God's* work that muft not be undone, tho' it had better never have been done at all? But being done, why muft all natural means of relief be debarr'd? Sure this *prohibition* is a demonftration of *hardnefs of heart* with a witnefs, It feems to me, that it had been equally reafonable, if this precept had been given, Whom God has made miferable by pains, poverty, ficknefs, difeafe, or wretchednefs of any kind, let no man help or relieve ; becaufe it is God's doing. This, I think, would have been juft as good, right, humane and reafonable.

Did *Mofes* write the precept of divorce to the *Jews*, becaufe of *the hardnefs of their hearts* ; and was this precept the cure for that malady ? Why then did *Jefus* forbid it ? If it was no cure, why did *Mofes* give it ? Or, did God give it as a trial for a cure, as a phyfician in an unknown and unaccountable diftemper gives remedies by guefs, and when he finds the prefcription ill applied, or not anfwering the end, forbids the taking it ? Men muft be very ftupid to affert this. But if this was not the cafe, or fomething like it, why did God command at one time, what he forbad at another? This is making God a mere Empiric, whofe conduct is directed by practice and experience ; and when his own experiments are not figned with *probatum eft*, he depends on that of others. When men cannot fee things invifible within the human body, they may be nonplus'd · But if God made man's frame and conftitution, he muft needs know what infirmities and failings he has made him liable to, and how to apply a proper remedy, if he is Almighty and All-wife.

This precept of divorce appears as much to be the law of God by *Mofes*, as any other laws given by *Mofes* were, (the Ten Commandments excepted ;)

ed ;) for *Moses* does not appear to have been compelled to give this precept as a permission by the
obstinacy of his nation, against his own judgment ;
and as there are not the least appearances of reason
to ground this conjecture on, so there is no reason
to believe, that any thing like it was the motive
which induced him to grant this indulgence ; or,
that he gave it by connivance, as a permission, rather than a law.

This *hardness of heart* being constitutional from
certain causes, Why did the physician of souls forbid *hard hearts to be mollified with this* Mosaic *ointment* of divorce ? *Is there no balm in* Gilead, *is
there no physician there ? Why then is the health of
the daughter of my people* forbid to be *recovered ?*

The gracious Lord *Jesus* was no enemy to the
Adulteress, who was taken *in the very act* ; for he
pleaded her cause in so friendly a manner, as tho'
it had been the least of all sins ; * *He that is without sin among you* (said he) *let him first cast a stone
at her.* Probably *Christ* knew the circumstances
of her adultery, and her penitence and humility to
be such, as render'd her worthy his being her *Ad-
vocate* ; and this might have been a trap laid against
her life, seeing she was caught in the very act ; tho'
the historian don't acquaint us with the circumstances. The evangelical writers give very lame
and imperfect accounts of things ; which have given
room for many alterations, interpretations, and in-
terpolations: Though, these things considered, this
precedent is not to be taken as an encouragement
to *adultery,* as tho' it was the least of all sins ; yet,
I think, we may make this application of it, not to
condemn those that are guilty of this *innocent adultery* (if it must be called adultery), of putting away
a tormentor, and taking a delightful companion in
room thereof.

Or

* *John* viii. 7.

Or do thefe words, *for the hardnefs of your hearts*
Mofes *wrote you this precept*, mean, that it was
neceffary men fhould be indulged in this liberty in
putting away their wives, left if they were debarr'd they would be hard-hearted to them, and
treat them very ill? If this be what thefe words
mean, the reafon remains good ftill , becaufe men
are not changed, their hearts are as hard as ever;
the Gofpel has not foftned them at all . Then the
law is good ftill, and founded on good reafon.
Divorces were allowed to prevent worfe confequences, which is the intention of all good laws,
they are given to prevent the greater evils, for the
beft cannot prevent ALL bad confequences , becaufe good and evil are fo intermixt and inter-
woven into the nature of things, that laws for a
publick or general good, are productive of fome
particular evils , and laws enacting things injurious to the public, are productive of good to
fome particular perfons   If *Mofes* gave a command that men fhould put away the wives they
difliked, to prevent their being hard-hearted to
them, and ufing them cruelly or unjuftly , *Mofes*
enacted a good law, which it is evil to annul , and
then prohibiting divorces, is a hard-hearted and
cruel prohibition, unjuft in its nature, and evil in
its confequences.   And if men are to be known,
as a tree by its fruits, no good man could bring
forth fuch evil fruits, as to repeal this excellent
law, given to foften the hard heart of man.

Becaufe of the hardnefs of your hearts Mofes
wrote you this precept.   Therefore it was a proper
means to foften hard hearts, which would have
been cruel had they been deprived of all means of
cure: As with us, where the poor have no remedy but death, which defperate remedy makes the
difeafe defperate. " The nature of man is ftill
" as weak, and their hearts are as hard as ever,

E   " and

" and that weakness and hardness as unfit and un-
" tractable to be harshly used as ever. Seeing
" therefore that all the causes of any allowance
" that the *Jews* might have, remain as well to
" the Christians. This is a certain rule, that as
" long as the causes remain, the allowance
" ought."

But from the beginning it was not so. If this be
a rule to determine and distinguish, what are the
laws of God, and what of *Moses*, then 'tis a rule
to determine other laws by, whether they are
from God or no, by whomsoever they are given,
viz. the laws of God for the government of human
nature existed with man, and is imprinted in him, and
then there is no other law than natural reason and
fitness, consequently all laws are to be referred to
this. If nothing can be the law of God, which
from the beginning was not so. If the laws of
God are known by their being before *Moses*, and
consequently independent of him, they are also before *Jesus*, and independent of him, the one could
not make them, or make them known, which
were not made or known before, nor the other
make them void. Then all the laws of God are as
irrevocable, as the general course of things and human nature as unchangeable.

'Tis said in old time, *the sons of God saw the
daughters of men, and took them wives of all they
liked*; and undoubtedly they put away all they did
not like: For as their own liking was the rule
of their choice, consequently their disliking was
the rule for their refusal, both before chusing and
after: For when man is left at liberty to act according to nature, the liking and disliking will
always be his distinguishing rule of choice and refusal in all things, but in nothing more so, than in
embracing a woman for a wife; he cannot do o-
therwise, unless he is compelled by some greater necessity,

cessity, which destroying his free power of election and rejection must consequently destroy his happiness. Therefore to say concerning divorce, *from the beginning it was not so*, is not true; for from the beginning that it could be so, it was so.

And I say unto you, whosoever shall put away his wife, except it be for fornication, and shall marry another, committeth adultery; and whoso marrieth her that is put away, doth commit adultery. St. Mark *adds, if a woman shall put away her husband, and be married to another, she committeth adultery.*

St. *Mark* tells us, that the Disciples at another time ask'd him about this matter, and received an absolute answer, without a reason to enforce or explain it, and they seemed to be content with it; for *Jesus taught them as one having authority, and not as the Scribes:* 'Tis likely therefore, that they reasoned, but his *ipse dixit* was sufficient, considering his person, as it carried the more authority with it. *I say unto you*, is an authoritative expression. *Verily, verily*, were the two witnesses to attest the truth of what he said, and the reasons to illustrate it.

Absolute authority may command or pronounce what it pleases, but cannot make that wrong which in the nature of things is right, or that right which in the face of reason is wrong; which is the rule for all men to judge of right and wrong by, but to those who know not the use of reason, any thing may be right or wrong, good or evil: for those that have not a right rule to judge by, can never form a right judgment of men and things. Arbitrary power may be most proper to be exercised in governing mad men and fools, but rational creatures can submit only to the authority of reason, in determining what are just and unjust actions; therefore with all such, a mandate or sentence

void

void of reason, is void of authority; and that to which none is joined, or can be underftood, but the will and pleafure of the fpeaker, will only be regarded or rejected as his peculiar power or wifdom is, or is conceived to be, to inforce it But to a man that judges reafonably of things, a command without reafon, is no command at all, and, contrary to reafon, is to be defpifed, and ought not to be obeyed.

Reafon or common fenfe, is that rule by which all rules are to be tried, the indelible law of human nature, prior and fuperior to all laws, which whatever cannot ftand the teft of, is evidently wrong If arbitrary law, without reafon, and even againft reafon be right, any impofition is right; and one bare affertion is equal to another, when no reafon is given for either. That which does not carry its own reafon with it till the reafon be difcovered, is no law It can bind no further than lawlefs power binds it 'Tis not the perfon but the reafon makes the law, for law is always confidered as founded on reafon, without this 'tis not properly law or juftice, but oppreffion and injuftice. This inftead of healing the little diforders in the body politic, is fuch a quack medicine as fixes it in the blood, which makes a cut a gangrene, converts a flight cold or indigeftion to a malignant fever, or a flight fever to a mortal plague or deadly infection, and all that make abfolute irrational laws, are political quacks; who, to fay the beft that can be faid of them, are evidently ignorant of human nature. Is undivorcible matrimony, when miferable, the *ycke that is eafy, and the burden that is light*, which we are call'd upon to take on us? Or, can this doctrine be recommended as fuch?

It is a queftion what the word *fornication* in the text, means. Some think it fignifies uncleannefs,

nefs, and refer to the fenfe of the law. *When a man hath taken a wife and married her, and it come to pafs fhe find no favour in his eyes, becaufe he hath found fome* uncleannefs *in her* But if our fpiritual doctors and dictators take the word *fornication* in its right fenfe, it is ftrange to me, that it is not rather called *adultery*; for *fornication* is explained to be the act of copulation of unmarried perfons. But if a married woman be guilty of this act with any other man than her hufband, it is term'd *adultery*; fo that according to the common fenfe of the word *fornication*, a married woman cannot be guilty of it, unlefs it mean the action committed before marriage If this, and this only give right to a man to divorce his wife, then every man who marries one that has been tampering or trying with another beforehand, ought to have the liberty of divorce in his own power; but if Mr. *M———n* could have obtained this, it might have fav'd him much trouble, and fome thoufands of pounds expence, by the confeffion of his dear fornicatrefs *T——a C——a P——ps*. He is an inftance, that the moft religious men when hamper'd with a torment, will run any hazard to obtain the much defired redemption, and chufe with *David, rather to fall into the hands of God, than of man* or woman· And fhe is a proof that fome wives will drive men to hell, tho' they are fure to follow them in, rather than be divorced from their fubftance. And therefore the reafonablenefs of this liberty does moft evidently appear in all fuch cafes wherein it is moft ardently fought for.

If by the word *wife* here meant, is a woman join'd in wedlock to a man, to whom fhe is a deftroyer of his peace, his health and happinefs, of his goods and good name, not to put away fuch a wife, except for *fornication* (and we know not what that means) has neither reafon nor juftice in it.
This

This is not surely *Christ's coming into the world to redeem the world*, for it seems rather by this law as if he came to sentence the honest and suffering part of it to slavery and bondage, as long as their existence here lasts. This is *not to send peace on earth, but fire* to be kindled in the spirit of man, that shall burn up all his happiness. To sentence persons to dwell together till death, whose tempers are as opposite as light and darkness, heaven and hell, is to sentence their death and darkness as disconsolate and dismal as hell itself. Therefore if *Jesus Christ* was what he is said to have been, the *redeemer of mankind*, and did what he is said to have done, *preach deliverance to the captives, and set at liberty them that are bruised*, this prohibition of divorce, this preachment of slavery, and breaking the bruised reed, never came from him, and is not his doctrine.

We are at a loss to know what the sin of *fornication* means Mr JOHN MILTON says, it has some mystical meaning, and therefore conceives it to be that of *spiritual fornication*, which he defines to be, the wife's affections being alienated from her husband, and settled on another man, not on the man she has.

She that is thus divorced in soul, is not united to her husband mentally, and should be divorced bodily; for what is more contrary to the original institution than this? A disagreement in mind, and disobedience in action, much more breaks the marriage bonds than adultery. If a woman prostitute her body to her husband, when her soul is estranged from him, is this marriage? Is it not rather intrinsically whoredom in the worst sense of it, and a greater evil than *adultery?* " For no wise man but would sooner pardon the " act of adultery committed once and again by a
" person

" perſon worth pity and forgiveneſs, than wear
" out his ſpirits with one that is of an unſociable,
" unloving and a miſchievous diſpoſition ; who
" would commit adultery too, but for envy, leaſt
" the unhappy ſlave ſhould obtain his releaſe.
" Things that cauſe an irreconcilable offence,
" and are not capable of amendment, annihilate
" the bands of marriage, which adultery only
" breaks ; for that once paſt and pardoned, where
" it can be pardoned, may be amended ; but that
" which naturally diſtaſtes, and finds no favour in
" the eyes of matrimony, can never be concealed,
" never appeas'd, never intermitted, but proves
" a perpetual nullity of love and content. Natural
" hatred, whenever it ariſes, is a greater evil to
" marriage than the accident of adultery ; a greater
" defrauding, a greater injuſtice. He that knows
" not the truth of this, knows not what true love
" is A diſobedient and diſagreeable temper and
" behaviour much more breaks matrimony than
" the act of adultery, tho' repeated ; for this may
" be done, and not known, ſo not felt as a trou-
" ble ; and being known, may be repented of,
" and amended, and redeemed, with more ardent
" love and duty to the forgiving huſband ; but
" the fornication in affection, this dereliction of
" meetneſs and agreeableneſs of temper cannot be
" unknown, nor amended if it be natural, nor
" confeſſed or repented of. Beſides, an adultereſs
" may pleaſe in all her behaviour otherwiſe,
" but the behaviour of the other can never pleaſe
" in all ſhe does She defrauds him of all con-
" tentment, and enjoyment ; ſo that ſhe is leſs a
" wife than an adultereſs Neceſſary and juſt
" cauſes have neceſſary and juſt conſequences :
" What error and diſaſter join'd, reaſon and equi-
" ty ſhould disjoin."

I have been informed, that a gentleman had a wife who was an adulteress, and the husband was not unacquainted with her transgressions, yet loved her, because she was, as he said, very pretty, and very obliging in every thing else

" *He that putteth away his wife, except for for-*
" *rication,* that is, if it be this spiritual fornica-
" tion, the alienation of her affections, *causes her*
" *to commit adultery,* breaks off her affections to
' fix them on another man Carnal adultery is
" but transient injury compar'd with natural ha-
" tred, which is such an unspeakable offence and
" grief, as admits of no amends, no cure, no
" ceasing, but by divorce , this, like the divine
" *fiat,* in one moment gives life and harmony to
" the crude and discordant chaos, it hushes out-
" rageous tempests into sudden stillness and peace-
" ful calm He that binds together the dissensions
" of complaining nature in chains invincible,
" commits the adultery, not he that would sepa-
" rate them "

The utmost rigour of the literal sense does not forbid divorce, but *he that divorces and marries arother committeth adultery* Here's no prohibition not to put away a wife, there's no adultery in that The *Esseres* were great admirers of a single life, so that it was no crime to put away a wife and live single; but all the sin and all the devil was in marrying, and he that finds the devil in that state is willing to get rid of it at any rate, even on condition of not to marry again , there-fore divorces ought to be freely allowed It is not much to be wondered at, if a man in defence of his birth be no friend to marriage, whose mother that bare him was not married to his father that begat him. *She that putteth away her husband* (so called), *and marrieth again, committeth adultery; and he that marrieth her that is put*

away,

away, committeth adultery; but suppose the woman is cruelly used, or wrongfully divorced, and accepts the refuge and protection of an honester man, who would marry her, love her, and use her tenderly, how does she commit adultery, or he that marries her? Is *adultery* to be committed every way by the light as well as the dark parts, by humanity as well as inhumanity, by soft hearts as well as by hard hearts; adultery then is every thing committed by *adults*. Don't mistake me, I am far from encouraging adultery, either spiritual or carnal; either in Mr. MILTON's virtuous sense, or Mr. *Rake's* vicious one, but *adultery*, in any sense, which to me is absurd and ridiculous, cannot be approved of by my understanding. If the text be not strictly true in the plain literal sense, without the twisting art of a crafty expositor, it must be understood in a discretional, moral and parabolical sense; but to be discretionally understood, this with a little *moralising* the text, or *merding* it, seems consistent with reason, *viz.* He that putteth away his wife, without any just cause, but merely to marry another, committeth adultery; and the man that putteth them asunder, or is the cause of it, that he may marry her that is put away, being thus accessary thereto, committeth adultery. This seems reasonable and therefore right, " the condi-
" tions not being express'd yet wanting in reason,
" are to be understood."

No man's character, perhaps, has ever suffered such excess of contempt and honour, as that of *Jesus Christ*, some in his life-time esteemed him a *devil,* and a mad-man, for they said, * *He is a devil and is mad, why hear ye him?* Other men, at other times have esteemed him a God, and set him in the throne of the most high. The true character of such a person 'tis very hard to know. Had he wrote his doctrines himself, we might have had some

F   rule

* *John* x. 20.

rule whereby to judge of them and him ; but inftead of this, we have only bad collections of fome
things reported to be faid and done by him, of
doubtful original; the fentences are often without
coherence or connexion; and for the moft part
fo very ambiguous, that his fincereft followers are
everlaftingly puzzled how to underftand them ;
tho' they educate men in learning, and keep them
in pay, on purpofe to expound thofe myfterious
writings. And as little efficacious is the illumina-
tion of the *fpirit* to thofe that think they *fee* its
light, and *feel* its operations; therefore the
fincereft followers of *Chrift* are everlaftingly divided into fects, and rent into factions. The more
literally abfurd or dark the matter is, fo much
more are their underftandings clouded and con-
founded about them ; and by how much more neceffary they apprehend the true underftanding of
them to be, by fo much the more are they in defperate earneft, and daggers draw about them. I
think, the giving doctrines and precepts to the
common people for their common information and
conduct, that are out of the reach of common fenfe,
highly reflects on the wifdom and goodnefs of the
giver: But this difcourfe feems not to be of that
fort, tho' the more it be examined, the lefs juft
and reafonable it appears.

*His Difciples fay unto him, If the cafe of a man
be fo with his wife, it is not good to marry.* This,
in my opinion, is true , and fo (as we read) *Chrift*
acknowledged it to be ; for *He faith unto them,
All men cannot receive this faying, fave they to whom
it is given:* But if *all* men cannot receive this
faying, furely it was not given to be received
by all men ; and therefore ought never to pafs into a law for all to obey. The truth of this ftory
is incredible, becaufe he had *women difciples*, that
he fhould be fo much againft marrying, as to recommend

mend by the following words *mutilation* rather, that he whom nature has not qualified to live in an unmarried state, should qualify himself by the knife, and cut out his way to the kingdom of heaven, which, if this admonition or advice leads to, *suffers violence, and the violent take it by force.*

The goodness of the lawgiver does not make the law good, but rather shews how good the lawgiver is ; even respecting the great lawgiver God himself, it may be said, laws are not good because God commands them ; but God commands them, because they are good. Otherwise authority, not goodness, are the motives of his law. He commands us to regulate our dispositions for our own good, but not to destroy ourselves, or mutilate our members, which would make religion worthy of abhorrence, a detestation and plague to mankind, and the sanctified destruction of all human happiness.

In *Genesis*, the Father says, *It is not good that man should be alone.* In *Matthew*, the Son seems to say, *It is best for man to be alone.* God says, *I will make a help meet for him.* By his Son's doctrine, *It is better for a man to dismember himself than accept of her.*

For there are some eunuchs, which were so born from their mother's womb, and there are some eunuchs which are made eunuchs of men ; and there be eunuchs which have made themselves eunuchs for the kingdom of heaven's sake : He that is able to receive it, let him receive it. These words have been thought by some to have a different meaning, than what they seem to have in the letter ; but 'tis probable, the reason why some think so, is, because the old maxim seems by this to be reviv'd : *Ezek* xx, 25. *I gave them also statutes that were not good, and judgments whereby they should not live.* What doctrine can be more destructive of human happiness and human kind, than this ? Tho' if 'tis to

F 2   be

be differently underſtood, no man can be certain
what is the certain meaning of theſe words.
This doctrine, that *it is good for a man not to
marry*, is ſuch as *all men cannot receive*. Eunuchs
may, elſe why are they named? And in order that
men may receive it, they are recommended to
make themſelves *eunuchs*, if they are not ſo made
by nature, nor by men; elſe what mean theſe
words that are ſubjoin'd, *He that is able to receive
it, let him receive it?* If the words have ſome ſpi-
ritual meaning, how ſhall we know what that meaning is? The diſciples never aſked him, they ſeem-
ed to have been credulous and un-enquiring ſouls,
and to have received almoſt all things implicitly;
for when they knew they could not underſtand
what their maſter ſaid to them, they were a-
fraid to aſk him [*]. So they were like to profit
much by *his* teaching, and we by *theirs*.

   Suppoſe there are ſome men born *eunuchs*, and
others ſo made, and cannot commit adultery;
what then, are they ever the better for this imbe-
cility? And if ſome men have been fools enough
to make themſelves ſo, for the kingdom of
heaven's ſake, are they ever the nearer the kingdom of heaven for ſo doing? If they are not, why
is the exhortation annex'd, *He that can receive it,
let him receive it?* But alas! the *women!* what
muſt they do, is it proper for them to be ſpaded?
The Popiſh prieſts however, that pretend not to
defile themſelves with women, let them be made
geldings of, that they defile not women. Surely
it is not improper to practiſe this upon them, that
thoſe who teach the way to heaven may not miſs
of it themſelves, for the good of their own ſouls,
and the ſouls of their female penitents. If this
law was made and put in execution, it might do
well to prevent the ſpirit of popery and rebellion
                                              from

[*] *Mar.* ix 32.

from exerting itfelf, and to preferve proteftant liberty among us

If the *letter fenfe* is unjuftifiable, I fear it is too palpable for the *fpirit* to hide, nor can I fee that it will bear a *fpiritual* fenfe, without making it matter of ridicule : forafmuch as there is not the appearance of *fuch* a meaning in it; for if *part* of this anfwer of *Chrift* to the Pharifees be *fpiritual,* why not the *whole* ? If part be, then men afk a natural queftion, and receive a fpiritual anfwer, which if it be *hiftory,* and not all a *parable,* is abfurd. If *Chrift*'s anfwer be myftical to the Pharifees plain queftion ; is it not like the nonfenfe or crofs purpofes in *Erafmus,* where one talks of a *wedding,* and the other of *fhipwrack ?* Alas ! for believers, all their refuge is in myftery, and all their fafety lies in obfcurity. If thefe words of *Chrift* are to be *myftically* underftood, be ye in labour ye *fpiritual mothers* of the Church, bring forth and reveal the myftery, and defend it by reafon, or your fpiritual *wifdom* and *power* will be meanly thought of. If the *whole be myfterious,* the letter is no law ; and if it pafs into a law, it is unjuft ; for if the letter is to be differently underftood, if it want explaining or amending, fo muft the law do that is founded upon it.

He that can, or thinks he can, explain the fenfe, or vindicate the *humanity* of the expreffion, fo as to prove the doctrine righteous, and the precept good, let him do it, and all due regard fhall be paid to the reafons that are given. Let him difplay his abilities in explaining or vindicating this fpiritualizing precept; and deliver us from the dilemma it involves us in. If none can be found that can do this ; but if he that bravely attempts, fhamefully fails in his endeavours ; let him *lay his hand upon his mouth,* or *his mouth in the duft,* and confefs that *he cannot order his fpeech by reafon of darknefs.*

For my part, I own, that the best method I can perceive to justify *Jesus Christ*, is, by confessing there are errors in St. *Matthew's Gospel*, especially such *parts* of it are faulty, as are indefensible by plain and honest reasoning, and are not confirmed by the other Gospels. To be too stiff in this point, in defence of the whole, is to destroy the whole, which, according to what we read, is not Gospel policy. *Mark* ix. *If thine hand or foot offend thee, cut it off; or, if thine eye offend thee, pluck it out; it is better for thee to enter into life maimed, or halt, or with one Eye; than having two hands, two feet, or two eyes, to be cast into hell.* As such like expressions in this place are sentences independent of what goes before and after; so they are capable of being explained in whatever sense the *Church* pleases. But if the subject going before and after such words in *St. Matthew*, are to direct us to their meaning, it seems to point to this doctrine of Castration. *Mat.* v. *ver* 27 to 32. *Ye have heard that it hath been said by them of old time, Thou shalt not commit adultery. But I say unto you, that whosoever looketh on a woman to lust after her, hath committed adultery with her already in his heart. And if thy right eye offend thee, pluck it out, or hand, cut it off, and cast it from thee; for it is profitable for thee, that one of thy members should perish, and not that thy whole body should be cast into hell. It hath been said, whosoever will put away his wife, let him give her a bill of divorcement. But I say unto you, whosoever shall put away his wife, saving for the cause of fornication, causeth her to commit adultery; and whosoever shall marry her that is divorced, committeth adultery.* Concerning the first part of these words, I think, unless a man look on a *married woman* to lust after her, he *does* not commit *adultery* in his heart. Besides, a man may look on a woman to lust after her in an honourable manner, as the law allows, or natural reason permits; and he cannot for so doing be properly said to *commit adultery in his heart*

Concerning that part of advising *to dismember the body*, if it has not an eye to *eunuchism*, I know not what it means; nor can the *preceding* and *subsequent* words direct us to the meaning of it. And as to the latter part of these words concerning *divorce*, the exceptions against it, are neither *small* nor *few*. But my present business is with the *amputation* part, to be executed on the *parts of generation*, which naturally causes these unhappy questions, or reflections, permit me the freedom of mentioning some of them.

" Advising men to *make themselves eunuchs for*
" *the kingdom of heaven's sake*, is as scandalous a
" doctrine, and as ill-judged sanctity, as ever was
" preached to the world. An Atheist disbelieves
" a God, because he finds fault with the order of
" nature; if an Author of religion does the same,
" he sows the seeds of Atheism He grants the
" causes of Atheism who proposes an unnatural
" remedy to rectify nature; and the consequence
" that the world is not the production of *Wisdom*,
" naturally and necessarily follow."

If this be the way to *enter into* LIFE, to cut off the *members*, or means of it, it is no wonder that *strait is the gate, and narrow is the way, and few there be that find it* Is the practice of this doctrine, *eating the bread of life*, which cuts off all life? Or, does he *give life to the world*, whose doctrines, if put in practice, cuts off the life of the world? Is not this like men's devouring their offspring, after the example of the old heathen God *Saturn?* May not his own question to the Pharisees be retorted on him, *Is it lawful to save life, or to destroy it?* Is not recommending the *piety* of this practice, like re-

commending

commending * the *wisdom* of the *unjust steward?* Is
there any natural *piety* or *wisdom* in it? If it be supernatural, is not supernatural piety, impiety, or impracticable? And supernatural wisdom, incompre-
hensible or nonsense? Is this a doctrine or precept
becoming *the Saviour of the world* to teach? Is the
way to *destroy* the world, the way to *save* it? Is
not this the most *unmanly* advice that ever was
taught mankind? Which, if all men practised,
would end the world as to the human species?
What a *lover of mankind* must he be thought to
be, that teaches to extirpate all human race? If
Christ spoke without dissimulation, *not* teaching
one thing, and meaning another; or, if the contrary, what a mean opinion will men conceive of
him, if this expression be his? *Some have made
themselves eunuchs for the kingdom of heaven's sake:
He that can receive it, let him receive it?* For in
any sense to ascribe it to *Jesus Christ*, brings dishonour to his name. *Women* must by this appear to
be, or be look'd upon, as the greatest evils in nature, and ths must induce them to hate and abhor
men: For to be married to their Saviour, will not
satisfy their wants. No person preaching such
morals, can so *sanctify* them, as such morals can
unsanctify his person. *Good and evil*, are founded
in the nature of man, and man's wisdom finds and
applies them by the fitness or unfitness of things,
and regulates his actions by their tendency; but
folly runs counter to the course of nature, and directs men to act contrary to it. If a single life be
so holy a thing, that men are recommended *for
the kingdom of heaven's sake*, to make themselves
eunuchs, rather than marry; why then, if married,
ought they not to be divorced for the kingdom of
heaven's sake, when for the sake of all happiness
on earth they earnestly desire it? Or is it *then* only good, when it is so bad, that it cannot be borne,

because

* *Luke* xvi 8.

becaufe *then* it is the moft *mortifying* ftate ? Or, is divorce abfolutely forbidden (in all cafes but fornication) to make the married ftate the more grievous to be endured, to deter men from entering into it ?

I fee but one way to remove thefe objections, and get over thefe difficulties, and that way feems natural and eafy, where it is not barr'd up by bigotry and prejudice again ft natural reafon, which informs me, that as *St. Mark* has not mentioned this expreffion, who relates the difcourfe, it ftands upon the fingle credit of *St. Matthew*, and confequently the reafon for believing it, is rendered the weaker. And as *Jefus Chrift* did not write it himfelf, to believe it came not from him, is not difbelieving him, nor any thing difhonourable of him, who tells us in a parable, *Mat.* xxiii. that *after the feed of the word was fown, the enemy would fow tares among it*. And it feems to me that nothing is more apparent, than that many Chriftians, have from the beginning of Chriftianity to this day, father'd their own wild and ftupid opinions on *Chrift*, of which he was not the author ; and that this expreffion at leaft, if not the whole difcourfe, is an *interpolation of the monks*, who have had the fecret management of thefe books ; this doctrine being fitted to recommend their kind of life ; the Gofpels being kept in a private manner for more than *three hundred years*, will allow of this conjecture. If the hiftorians, whoever they were, faid that they were eye or ear witneffes, we have only their own *unknown evidence*, to fupport their teftimony. But the *doctrines* and *precepts* delivered in the Gofpels are better known, how divine they are, by their own clearnefs, natural tendency, and ufefulnefs, than by any thing that can be faid about them. Light and truth difplay themfelves.

G

Of Divorce, *and* Cohabiting Unmarried.

IT makes mifery, which would be tolerable if cur-
able, to be intolerable if incurable ; at leaft it
adds mifery to mifery, to think it cannot end but
with life, or at the pleafure of another, who in-
flexibly purfues that pleafure, which is my pain,
and I cannot prevent it. This may be the too late
reflections of a man diftreffed by wedlock : My wife
Demonia (cries he) vindicates her honour at the expence of mine, fhe has a tongue form'd for deceit,
without its being perceiv'd ; and by this infcruta-
ble art, can blaft even the character of an angel.
There appears to be no hypocrify in her, becaufe
it is fo natural, that it feems to be artlefs If I
grant her not all fhe requires, fhe will privately
obtain it, both for pleafure and expence ; and this
fecret management is my fure ruin. I am déter-
mined to oppofe it might and main ; now my
houfe is filled with eternal brawl and clamour !
and thro' all my neighbourhood, with whom I had
once reputation and refpect, infamy and fcandal
attend me ! My dear name, my facred character
is facrificed, and I am look'd upon to be the guilty perfon, wherever her malice finds admittance,
or her report flies. What fhall I do ? My once
joyous hours are fled, which I found in *Celeftia*'s
arms ; happinefs is no more ; a fullen ftar threat-
ens the remainder of my wretched life with diftrefs, not to be remedied by complaint or action :

A

A difmal gloom and melancholy view is all around me: She that ought to be both by intereft and gratitude my trueft comfort in diftrefs, and like a good confcience my chief fupport and folace in affliction, is my only grief and calamity ! O remedilefs ftate ! whither fhall I fly ? What fhall I do ? If I go, fhe, like a *malus genius* having no fupport but from me, will find me out and follow, and fpread the invenom'd flander of her lies and malice beyond my flight ; and whither can I go from the means of my fubfiftence ? I may as well finifh at once a wretched life, as attempt to fly the wretchednefs of it ; the difmal confequences of endeavouring to mend it, fhew me to be compleatly wretched, and plung'd, for ever plung'd, as into the gulph of gloomy *Tartarus*, where falling, I muft fall for ever ! O *Celeftia*, when I think of thee, I behold happinefs at an unapproachable diftance, like *Dives* in hell, with an unpaffable gulph between me and that, doubly damn'd with the lofs of fenfible happinefs, and a pungent fenfe of never-ceafing pain, but with life itfelf Adieu all the pleafures that I once embrac'd in embracing *Celeftia*, and any death is welcome. Is this the reward of my virtue ? O ye cruel gods, could ye not lengthen out my tranquillity to the end of a fhort tranfitory life ; or at leaft abate fo much of your undeferv'd vengeance, as not to have given me this torture for miftaken pleafure, which only the integrity of life and fincerity of my foul has made permanent ? Much could I fay, but much rather would I conceal her fhame, who is the caufe of my lamentation : When nature can no longer bear reftraint, fhe breaks thro' all oppofition. Tho' fome time fince kind fate has removed the painfulnefs of the fting by a much defired, but little expected and abfolutely neceffary feparation, the *third* time ; fo that *Demonia*, tho' living yet,

G 2

her

her nature defperately inimical to mine, offends me not; yet thefe paft reflections I remember ftill, my former *affliction and mifery, the wormwood and the gall**.

Thefe melancholy reflections, may be fuppofed, made to warn others, as the criminal with the gibbet in view prefents the fpectators with his laft dying fpeech. *Fœlix quem faciunt aliena pericula cautum.*

The want of liberty and redrefs in juft caufes of matrimonial complaints. changes the ftate of marriage defigned for a bleffing, into a curfe and captivity. However holy matrimony may be called, it is when unhappy much more unholy than whoredom, being productive of greater fin and mifery; becaufe this wretched ftate, hateful in its nature, and difmal in its confequences, is like the laws of the *Medes* and *Perfians*, unalterable but by death; and not to be abrogated like the laws of *Mofes*, tho' *they* are faid to have been by God's appointment, as well as matrimony. This unmerciful reftraint, without refuge or redemption, is the tyrannical effect of religious fuperftition. When once the facred knot is tied, and the matrimonial rites confummated. let the married perfons find themfelves ever fo much miftaken in their difpofitions and conftitutions of body and mind, by reafon of any matters mifunderftood, or not before known or expected, or in embrio, and impoffible to have been forefeen, tho' a cloud of gloominefs gathers thick, and veils all profpect of fucceeding happinefs, tho' perpetual difcord breaks in like an overflowing deluge; tho' malignant jealoufy infects the mind, and concealed leprofy or *lues* the body of either party, tho' envy poffefs the heart, venom and flander the tongue, diftorted rage and fury the face; tho' drunkennefs befot the head of

of the man or woman, or extravagance foreboding
sure ruin be his or her fatal conduct, or a multitude of vexations and plagues befides, too dread-
ful to name, too numerous to recount; tho' all
or fome of thefe, for all woes cannot find place
to wound one perfon, diforder and torment the
married ftate; tho' nothing remains but an un-
fpeakable diffatisfaction and defpair of every focial delight, the law, the terrible law of judgment
without mercy, and without end, has confign'd the
married, the marr'd, the miferable wretches over
as to a ftate of reprobation infupportable and ir-
redeemable; fo that the ideas of hell eternal, and
vengeance everlafting, does not make fuch a fenfible impreffion in human minds, as the fenfation
of this prefent calamitous condition : For, as that
is the greater pain which is the moft felt, fo it is
moft regarded, and makes the impreffion fo large,
that it effaces in a great meafure, if not entirely,
all leffer impreffions; when, let a man turn which
way he will, he fees pain and vexation, ruin and
deftruction tread every way before him that he can
turn ; fo that the goads of unjuft calumny and reproach torment his life, with defpicable poverty
in view, and a jail, a halter, or ftarving, bid fair
to *end* an uncomfortable life , tho' terrible be the
way to it, yet the word *end* tho' with *life*, is the
only comfort and confolation.

Good God ! that ever man or woman fhould
oblige themfelves by law to do what is not in their
own power, *viz* to love, when reafon, nature and
neceffity oblige them to hate, is fuch a ftate of
complaifant conformity and abject flavery, as one
would think a rational foul would not be guilty
of; but what will not tyrant cuftom on one hand,
with a profpect of the joys of love on the other,
oblige a man to do ? However eafy or tolerable
the chains may appear to be at a diftant profpect,
they

they that have dragg'd them with an unmerciful
clog, or rather load of woe, at the end, (which
when felt exceeds all their former conceptions)
find no state to be more difmal, no condition more
wretched, being doubly curs'd like the damn'd in
hell, with the fight of happinefs at a diftance enjoyed by others, and once hoped for by them,
which fair fky being overclouded they are now deprived of happinefs even in expectation, fo that,
there remains not even *hope* (that bubble comfort)
left, and in room of the once expected focial enjoyment, they feel lafting torment and fubftantial
woe.   No tender pity is fhewn, no bowels of compaffion extended to them that have unwarily or un-
fortunately plung'd themfelves into this inextrica-
ble mifery.   Matrimony, like death, is a great
leap in the dark ; only the one renders us fenfible
of our mifery, the other terminates our mifery in
infenfibility, at leaft in *body* till the fon of man
comes, *the day and hour whereof no man knows*;
nor that it is yet, or ever will be fixed, at leaft
he appears not likely to come till Chriftianity be
gone, for *when the fon of man comes fhall he find
faith on the earth?* And if he finds no faith on
earth, he will not find Chriftianity there ; for this
is built on that.
 If it be objected, that for adultery and impoten-
cy the law has provided a remedy ; this law is fo
fevere, and fo difficult to obtain juftice by, that
many who even by the tenor of that law have a
right to freedom, cannot find the means to attain
the end, it being attended with exceffive charges ;
and thofe whofe abilities prevent them not, chufe
rather from the humanity of their tempers, and the
modefty of their difpofitions, to fubmit to an uncomfortable life in mifery all their days, than
bring themfelves or their partners to lafting fhame,
and be recorded with difgrace, by having the matter

ter litigated before a public court, to the fcandal of both parties. The law fhould relieve the oppreffed, by means within the power of the oppreffed to find; and religion fhould not contribute to add a weight to oppreffion, and make it durable as life; but both fhould unite their inftructions and authority, to make the yoke of life eafy, and the burden light.

I fhall now give you the fubftance of Mr. JOHN MILTON's arguments for divorce, who was as excellent a reafoner as a poet.——He fays, that they who bring liberty to the much-wrong'd and griev'd ftate of matrimony, deferve to be reckoned among the public benefactors of civil and human life above the inventors of wine and oil; they fhall raife many helplefs Chriftians from the depth of fadnefs and diftrefs, utterly unfitted as they are to ferve God or man; they fhall fet free many daughters of *Ifrael*, not wanting much of her fad plight, whom Satan had bound eighteen years. Man they fhall reftore to his juft dignity and prerogative of nature, preferring the foul's free peace before the promifcuous draining of a carnal rage: Marriage from a perilous hazard and fnare, they fhall redeem to a more certain haven and retirement of happy fociety. When the grave and pious reafons of this law of divorce hath been amply difcours'd, I doubt not (*fays he*) but with one gentle ftroking to wipe off ten thoufand tears out of the life of man

He adds, That maintaining the reafonablenefs of divorce is attempting the cure of an inveterate difeafe, crept into the beft part of human fociety, which tends to the redeeming and reftoring of none, but fuch as are the objects of compaffion, having in an ill hour hampered themfelves to the lofs of all quiet and repofe during life. That ufeful life might not be loft and wafte away under a

fecret affliction of an unconfcionable fize to human
ftrength, the mercy of the *Mofaic* law was graciouf-
ly exhibited : That this prudent law of divoice by
Mofes is full of moral equity, agreeable to the
laws of the wifeft men, and moft civiliz'd nations ; that many bad men have made bad ufe of
this law, it is eafy to believe, yet *Mofes* knew it was
better to fuffer the accidental evils which would
arife from hard-hearted men by this precept, than
that good men fhould lofe their juft and lawful
privilege of remedy   That if this overture of eafe
and recovery be obftinately difliked, what remains
but to deplore a hopelefs, helplefs condition! That
if the knot of matrimony may in no cafe be diffolv-
ed, except for adultery, all the burdens of the law
of *Mofes* are not fo intolerable : That no laws can
bind againft the defign of its inftitution, which
was to be an help meet for man, his folace and
delight.

He reafons, That no law can juftly engage a
blamelefs creature to its own miftaken perpetual forrow : That the fatisfaction of the mind
in marriage fhould be more regarded and provided
for, than the fenfitive pleafing the body ; for
without the former, the latter foon becomes unfavoury and contemptible : That tho' the Liturgy
exprefly fays, We muft not marry to fatisfy the
flefhly appetite, like brute beafts that have no underftanding ; yet the Canon fo runs, as if it
dreamt of no other matter than fuch an appetite to
be fatisfied· That thofe, who in marriage are dif-
appointed of the better part, *i e.* of agreeable
converfation and folace, and rather than live in
fadnefs think it better to part, are moved to divorce by a motive equal to the beft of thofe that
marry, and has not the leaft grain of fin in it:
That 'tis above the ftrength of human weaknefs
to find fatisfaction in the lonely ftate which they

are

are fallen into by the means they attempted to shun. That the more sober a person in such case is, the greater melancholy and despair it brings upon him; therefore it is, that many wedded persons are dejected; tho' they pretend other causes to conceal it, because they know no remedy. That an unsociable consort sometimes destroys the other by grief: By this means many a one consumes away in a joyless and disconsolate condition; therefore here charity should interpose and proclaim the most desired and acceptable freedom. What is life without the vigour of it in private or public enjoyment? Since life is to be preferred to marriage, and constraint to remain in unsuitable marriage may shorten or endanger life, the preservation of life demands a separation.

He urges, That the very being of the marriage-covenant is unfeigned love and peace, without which the marriage is hypocrisy. That since St. *Paul* says, 1 *Cor* vii *God has called us to peace not to bondage,* he who cannot love let him divorce. And since *love is the fulfilling of the law,* where love is wanting, the law of the marriage-covenant cannot be fulfilled. That when the chief end of an ordinance is frustrated for which it is ordain'd, it is annull'd and invalidated, and ceases of course unless it be otherwise renew'd and restored to its primitive institution. That an overstrictness in discipline causes it to be broken and brought into contempt. That man, by unhappy marriage is rendred unfit for the service of God, and all the duties of social life. That the children of such ill-join'd wedlock may be call'd *the children of wrath*; unhappy marriage as little conduces to sanctify them, as if they had been bastards

That those who having discern'd each other's disposition, which oftimes cannot be known till after matrimony, shall then find a powerful reluc-

tance

tance and recoil of nature on either fide, blafting
all the content of mutual fociety, are not lawfully
married. If all that is fair, all that is poffible has
been tried in vain, to accommodate the matrimonial difcords of thofe who by fome falfe bait have
been drawn together, that the fleeping enmities of
nature might awake to agony and ftrife later than
prevention could have wifhed; what folly is it
ftill to ftand combating and battering againft invincible caufes and effects with evil upon evil, till
either the beft of our days be lingred out, or end-
ed with wafting forrow. A perfon may miftake
in fixing love without experience, but cannot err
that finds juft caufe to hate by woeful experience.
Hatred is divifion, and when natural hatred (which
is of God) feparates, let no man, let no law force
them to live together. No laws can unite thofe
whom averfion loaths and avoids. No laws can
oblige to love, whom nature compels to hate; affection cannot be forced: A reafonable and natural diflike no laws can remedy   That if a difagreeable body be no incitement to wedlock, a difagreeable mind is an enemy to it. That nature
teaches to divide any limb from the body to fave
the reft, tho' it be to the maiming and deforming
of the whole; and to fever any member by inci-
fion, that is gangrene, and tends to the mortifying
the body; what if man and wife then are one flefh,
they ought to be feparated when neceffity requires
it?

He proceeds, That the law was never defigned
to protect bafenefs and injury, yet indiffoluable
matrimony but by death does this very thing, and
maintains a contract in direct violation to the defign of the law, the dignity of man, the honour
of matrimony, and the inflexible motives of tender nature and loving difpofition. A moft unjuft
contract maintained by violence ufurping over
                                        humanity.

humanity. That if the *Sabbath* was made for man, not man for the Sabbath, much more may it be said of *marriage*: God never sets the ordinance above the man for whom it is ordained. What was ever more made for man alone, and less for God, than *marriage*; and shall we load it with a cruel and senseless bondage utterly against the good of man?

He shews, That jarring and discord continually grating in harsh tune together, oft end in rancour and spite. That it would be less scandal, to divorce a natural disparity, than to link them together inevitably to kindle one another with hatred; who, if dissever'd, would be friends in any other relation. That there is as much cruelty in forbidding to divorce, as not to marry. Is the confinement for the trial of our patience; but what if it subvert our patience, and faith too? This is tempting God, by putting a yoke upon the neck of men; which neither former ages, nor the present are able to bear. That many marry or accept of an offer by the persuasion of friends, which proving a mistaken state of confinement and misery, both parties are thereby render'd unhappy: And forced marriages are such savage inhumanity, that 'tis next to assassination; pity as well as piety therefore pleads for their redress by divorce.

That the Apostle *Paul* says, *What communion hath light with darkness, or he that believes with an Infidel?* Matrimony is, or should be a state of the nearest and dearest communion; those then that have no more communion with each other, than light and darkness, from whatever cause it be, have broke the bonds of matrimony, or they were never in that state of communion; and if either way, the bonds are dissolved of course. If there be so little communion between a believer and an Infidel, that if the one has a mind to separate, a se-

paration

paration is granted· *If the unbelieving depart, let him depart.* Surely a believer is to have the fame privilege as an unbeliever, if there be no communion between them ; and if this liberty be granted where one is an Infidel, *becaufe God has called us to peace, and a brother or fifter is not under bondage in fuch a cafe ;* fuppofe the cafe worfe, that the man is *worfe than an Infidel,* one that *takes no care to provide for his family,* is not the bondage greater ? May not the woman have the liberty to be delivered from fo worthlefs a man ? Or, muft fhe ever drag the chain of flavery and miferable fervitude ? And, inftead of receiving any help from him, endure to be ftarv'd and robb'd and abus'd, without remedy or redrefs during life ? *He that cares not for his own houfe,* and *fhe* that does the fame, who is regardlefs of performing thofe focial duties which the matrimonial ftate require, whether he or fhe goes from it, or ftays in it, is no part of it, and as fuch ought to have no place in it Is this doctrine of paffive flavery on one fide, and unmerciful tyranny on the other, that perfons fhould be wedlockt together to their utter ruin and undoing, the doctrine of the Gofpel ? Does this bring *glory to God, peace on earth, and good will to men ?* Is this *the liberty in which Chrift has made us free,* that we are advis'd to *ftand faft in ?* A liberty to tyrannize, and a freedom to flavery ! Can any thing be fo ridiculous and contrary to common fenfe ?

By this delicate reafoning of Mr MILTON, it is evident, that a man and woman who are fitly compofed in harmonious unity, as if conducted by one foul to the helps and comforts of domeftic life, are the proper fubjects only of conjugal ftate, for thefe, and only thefe can be happy, if their outward circumftances permit them to be fo : But if, upon experience their natures are contrary or wide-

ly

ly different to each other, they are differently con-
stituted, and not made for each other, nor can men
make that to agree which God has made to disagree; therefore such joining is not of him. When
men and women therefore are joined together by
law, they ought to be joined lawfully, that is according to equity; by allowing a *proviso*, disunion
or divorce, when evil arises, which blasts all expected comforts. When the law does not provide
a remedy for what is remediable, it is not as it
ought to be, adapted to the exigency of cases, or
the fitness of things; it is not so well design'd as it
should be; therefore in such cases it is not, it cannot be kept, nor is it fit it should, being an unfit
law If when the benefit of divorce to unhappy
marriages is denied, *it is not good for a man to
marry*; then on the contrary, if it be good for a
man to marry, 'tis just and right that the benefit
of divorce should be freely allowed to all unhappy
marriages.

I shall now answer all such questions and objections that I know of, which are made against divorces: Most of which rather shew the ignorance
of men how to do right, who are long accustom-
ed to do wrong, than any arguments against the
reasonableness and rectitude of divorce

'Tis queried, *What are the proper causes of divorce ?*

Answer. Whatever makes the married state miserable; for marriage was, and should be designed
for the mutual happiness of man and woman; if
one of them is render'd unhappy by it, the means
fails of the end, the institution is perverted, and
ought to be annulled

'Tis demanded, *Who ought to have the power of
procuring a divorce, the man or the woman ?*

A

A. The oppreffed or unhappy party; for law and juftice confifts in relieving the injured, and fupporting the helplefs. The perfon that feels the mifery, is the proper perfon to feek redrefs

'Tis afked, *To whom fhould they feek it? Should we have a court of judicature on purpofe? Or may married people divorce themfelves whenever they pleafe, or think themfelves unhappy?*

A They that think themfelves unhappy, are fo; for the feat of happinefs lies in the fenfation of it. T ere is liberty for fingle perfons to marry when they pleafe; and feeing the divorce of un-happy marriage is as neceffary for the well-being of man, as marriage is; why fhould not the fame freedom be allowed for one as the other?

Obj. At this rate, a man may turn away his wife, or a woman may go away from her hufband, whenever either of them pleafes, which will only change the fcene of mifery And if done by a courfe of law, the trouble and charge will make it ruinous to their characters and fortunes. Therefore 'tis better that no divorce be allowed

A. I am not propofing a divorce fo eafy as the one, nor fo difficult as the other; but, as I faid before, to part, ought to be as eafy as to come tó-gether; therefore let it be done in the very fame manner, and with the fame folemnity to make it legal, and give a fanction to the act. Let them that are divorced be feverely punifhed if ever they come together again (as the law of *Mofes* forbids) which will prevent parting for every flight occa-fion Let the divorce be obtained by being pub-lifhed three times in the parifh church, where the parties live, or by a Licence from the Commons, to be regifter'd at the faid church. Let the charge be the fame as marrying. Let rafcally *Fleet* mar-riages be prohibited, and let them be declared null and void; and whoever is fo married, let it be

esteemed

efteemed as adultery or whoredom: Then this fhop for clandeftine marriages will be fhut up; and people will not be every day marrying and un-marrying. There cannot be then fo much vice in matrimony, as there is now. "If nature's refift-
"lefs fway in love or hate be once compell'd, it
"grows carelefs of itfelf, vicious, ufelefs to fiiends,
"unferviceable and fpiritlefs to the common-
"wealth. This *Mofes* rightly forefaw, and all
"lawgivers that ever knew man. When the rea-
"fon and perfuafion of the married friends to re-
"concile them fail, all conftraint by law againft
"nature renders them but the more miferable."
By the married perfons being publifhed in church, in order to be divoiced, as they are or fhould be in order to be married; their friends and neigh-bours will be apprifed of it, and may endeavour a reconciliation. By this means many a divorce may be prevented.

If a man deferts his wife, or a woman her huf-band, has not the deferter broke the matrimonial covenant? Why may not the place by fuch de-fertion be declared vacant, or be efteemed a good reafon for obtaining a divorce, as well in a mar-ried as in a polical ftate? The defertion leaves the deferted in a ftate of freedom, to take another in the room of the deferter. Thefe are revolution-principles; and the reafons that juftify the one, will alfo juftify the other. 'Tis no more adul-tery for the deferted to marry another, than it was rebellion in the ftate to elect another king in the room of him, by whofe defertion the throne was wifely declared vacant; tho' it was more vacant from his unfitnefs to reign, than from his abfence. The nation by experience found *James* the *Second* an unfit perfon to be king, therefore made a proper ufe of a proper opportu-nity to difcard him, and place one more worthy in

his

his room ; fo fhould a man or woman do, who is deferted by, or obliged to defert a domeftic plague, and abandon home becaufe of the tyranny, oppreffion and mifery that reigns there When the caufes and reafons are alike, the verdict and juftice fhould be executed alike. Such like cafes ought to be a fufficient reafon for divorce, without any officious or impertinent enquiry and canvaffing private affairs by a public court of juftice into the caufes that produce the refolutions for divorce, out of a facred regard to the reputation of either or both parties Themfelves are the beft judges of their own grievances, and as fit to judge for themfelves why they diflike, and fo part, as they were to judge for themfelves why they liked, and fo were joined together : And much more, becaufe the latter is often founded on fancy ; but the former is the refult of experience Therefore the parties concerned are fitter judges for themfelves than a court of judicature ; becaufe oftimes the caufes are fecret : and 'tis not fit that the unaccountable and fecret reafons of diffatisfaction between man and wife fhould be toffed about and judged by a judicial court As the myfteries of marriage fhould be always preferved with chaftity ; the caufes of private differences fhould not be divulged to public town-talk, to pleafe every giddy goffip or prating fool, who love to be ever meddling with other people's affairs that never concern them, and never by fo doing mend them, but often make them worfe. " The differences that arife in pri-
" vate life fhould be cured and put an end to, but
" not publifhed ; they are often fo deeply rooted
" in natural affections, as are not within the verge
" of law to tamper with. *Paulus Emilius* being
" afked, why he put away his wife, for no vifible
" reafon ? Said, holding out his fhoe on his foot,
" This fhoe is a *new* fhoe, and a *neat* fhoe ; and
" yet

" yet none of you know where it wrings me. In
" cafes wherein a man's own happinefs is concern'd,
" he alone is his own judge, no other can judge
" for him, what he approves or difapproves,
" what is agreeable or difagreeable, lovely or
" hateful to his nature and conflitution To de-
" fire to redrefs a grievance, is natural , but to be
" obliged to expofe what good-nature and pru-
" dence would fecrete, is barbarous Tho' it may
" be juft to expofe an adulterefs, by public pro-
" ceeding againft her at law ; yet 'tis a benefit to
" the guilty wife, to be difcharg'd without hav-
" ing her honour impeach'd, as many a hufband
" would chufe rather to do, by a filent di'miſſion.
" 'Tis much better to difcharge her thus, than to
" have her faults fcrutinized and expos'd, and
" made the jeft of a way trial " But the differences in divorce about dowries, jointures eftates,
&c. fhould be determined by law, or as the contracting parties fhall judge meet, or agree to before marriage   People generally know how to
make their own bargains, the law is only neceffary to make them perform the covenants they enter
into, or determine what fhall be right when none
are made, as when a perfon dies without making
his will   When the parties are fo divorced, it is
as reafonable and as neceffary they fhould marry
again, as it was before, if to them it appear fo ;
when a poffibility or profpect is before them of
living happier with other mates, whofe difpofitions
and circumftances are better fuited to the temper
of each. And the perfon that is moft able, fhould
keep the children after parting, if there are any,
or, as they otherwife agree about it For, I think,
the father and mother have equal right to the children of their own begetting If a man leaves a
woman as wealthy as he found her ; and if fhe be
as healthy, I fee no juft reafon fhe has to complain

l   for

for his parting with her. Since money gives power, and the management of affairs is an indication of wisdom, and 'tis power and wisdom that govern the world (and 'tis fit it shou'd), therefore that person, be it the husband or wife, that was before marriage possess'd of the right of substance, and to whom the business after marriage most properly belongs should have the right of divorce, that the substance may be preserv'd, and the family maintain'd. She that brings a man a fortune who had none, should have a power to divorce the man that she has taken for a husband, who is spending it as fast as he can, that she may save as much as she can of it. And he or she that is careful of the family, should have power to divorce the other party that takes no care of it, who is therefore an unfit member of it. Understanding and circum-spection denote wisdom, and wealth gives power, they that have these have the supreme right, and 'tis an ill government where these are divided or disagree.

From a good wife and a wise manager of affairs, none but a fool or a madman would desire to be divorc'd, and from a fool or a madman it can bring no sorrow for a woman to be separated. Let them that cannot agree together, part, then it may be seen on whose side the fault lies ; the world often misunderstands and misjudges things. The power of divorce wou'd keep many in tolerable behaviour both men and women whose behaviour is now intolerable.

An ingenious author has these three objections to divorce*. 1 " What must become of the children upon the separation of the parents, must they be committed to the care of a stepmother, and instead of the fond care and concern of a mother feel all the indifference or hatred of a

stranger

---

* Mr. *Hume*, in his Essays moral and political.

ftranger or an enemy? Thefe inconveniencies are fufficiently felt where nature has made the divorce by the doom inevitable to all mortals: And fhall we feek to multiply thefe inconveniencies by multiplying divorces, and putting it in the power of parents upon every caprice to render their pofterity miferable?"

A. We often follow vulgar errors, think and fpeak as others do without judgment and without knowledge. Not every ftep-mother proves unnatural, nor every mother has natural tendernefs to her own, and fome have too much partiality; which tends as much to the fpoiling of children, as too little. A ftepmother cannot be eafily fuppofed an *enemy* to a man's children, if fhe loves the man. Every mother is not fit to bring up a child, becaufe fhe is mother of it, for fhe may have fondnefs without prudence, as mothers too generally have, but prudence without fondnefs is better for the education of children, which a ftepmother may have, and if fhe have not, if fhe treats them as an *enemy*, the father of the children has the fame remedy againft her, as againft their mother, *a divorce,* which will tend to difpofe her to prudence and regulation of her conduct, therefore *pofterity will* not *be rendered miferable,* but rather better brought up by this means; nor are *inconveniences multiplied by divorce,* but very much leffened, tho' they cannot by *any* means in *all* cafes be abfolutely done away. Jangling and contentious parents are certainly lefs fit to educate children, tho' their natural offspring, than thofe that, being freed from the diftraction and confufion of jarring tempers, can regulate and govern themfelves, their affairs and their family, with an even temper of mind.

Again he argues, 2. " If it be true on the one hand, that the heart of man naturally delights in

I 2

liberty, and hates every thing to which it is confin'd; 'tis also true on the other hand, that the heart of man naturally submits to necessity, and soon loses an inclination, when there appears an absolute impossibility of satisfying it. These principles of human nature you'll say, are contradictory. But what's man but a heap of contradictions. Tho' 'tis remarkable that where principles are after this manner, contrary in their operation, they do not always destroy each other; but the one or the other may predominate on any particular occasion, according as circumstances are more or less favourable to it. For instance, love is a restless and impatient passion, full of caprice and variations, arising from a feature, from an air, from nothing, and suddenly extinguishing after the same manner. Such a passion requires liberty above all things; and therefore *Eloisa* had reason, when, in order to preserve this passion, she refused to marry her beloved *Abelard*.

How oft when prest to marriage, have I said,
Curse on all laws, but those that love has made:
Love free as air, at sight of human ties,
Spreads her light wings, and in a moment flies.

But *friendship* is a calm and sedate affection, conducted by reason and cemented by habit; springing from long acquaintance, and mutual obligations; without jealousies or fears, and without those feverish fits of heat and cold, which cause such an agreeable torment in the amorous passion. So sober an affection therefore as friendship, rather thrives under constraint, and never rises to such a height as when any strong interest or necessity binds two persons together, and gives them some common object of pursuit. Let us consider then, whether love or friendship should most predominate in marriage? And we shall soon determine, whether liberty or constraint be most favourable to it. The happiest marriages to be sure are found, where love by long acquaintance is consolidated into friendship. Whoever dreams of raptures and extasies beyond the honey-moon, is a fool. Even romances themselves, with all their liberty of fiction, are obliged to drop their lovers the very day of their marriage, and find it easier to support the passion for a dozen of years under coldness, disdain and difficulties, than a week under possession and security. We need not therefore be afraid of drawing the marriage knot the closest possible. The friendship betwixt the persons, where it is solid and sincere, will rather gain by it; and where it is wavering and uncertain, this is the best expedient for fixing it. How many frivolous quarrels and disgusts are there, which people of common prudence endeavour to forget, when they lie under the necessity of passing their lives together; but which would soon inflame into the most deadly hatred, were they pursued to the utmost under the prospect of an easy separation."

A. If the heart of man naturally delights in liberty, when the heart of man has what it delights in, man will be best pleased, and consequently retain the most agreeable temper of mind. It ruffles his temper to take that from him which his heart naturally delights in, this is the direct way therefore to make him a bad husband, and this is the reason that many men's love grow cold to their wives, as soon as they consider their loss of liberty, that alone changes their temper, and by this means they curse their fate, which they would otherwise bless. Love is the freest principle in nature, and is an enemy to confinement, therefore confinement is an enemy to love. It is no wonder then, that married people are generally miserable, the rea-

son

fon is plain, love and liberty go together. Love cannot be confin'd, no laws can fix it ; therefore *Eloifa*'s virtue is worthy the example of all women. She that would confine her hufband by law, does not feek his love, but fomething elfe ; fhe has the man, and perhaps his means, but rarely his love, for that no laws can bind ; love cannot fubmit to any fuch neceffity, tho' man may ; nor does neceffity to endure what man would avoid, alter the nature or inclination of man in reality, only in appearance. Suppofe a man is in prifon, and greatly defires liberty, but being well informed, that his ftate is fuch as it muft be for life, and that there's no reafon to expect the remedy he longs for, what then, is a prifon beft for him ? Or, does he grow pleas'd and delighted with his confinement ? Not at all. But when he finds that he cannot have the only relief that his foul wifhes for, as the only fuitable and agreeable one, he endeavours to feek fome other palliating remedy to mollify the feverity of his confinement, by taking to drink, or play, or converfation, or fome other thing whereby he *feems* to be fometimes delighted *in* his ftation, but he is never truly delighted *with* it, and he never lofes the inclination to liberty, but to appearance ; but if it may be fuppofed, that long time and cuftom has brought confinement to be more agreeable to him than freedom, it muft be, becaufe his fpirits having been fo really fubdued by long bondage, he wants the power of *enjoying* liberty if he had it ; he is now defpirited, and unfit for what he was before fit for in the ftate of freedom he before fo earneft'y long'd for, fo confinement to wedlock may in time make a man feem eafy concerning his ftate, but he rather feems than is fo, or he becomes carelefs and enervated, not affectionate and vigorous. A man that has a wound when he knows it

admits

admits no cure, if he has courage enough to support himself under the melancholy reflection, takes
what pleasure he can in life as long as it lasts,
knowing it will end his days, and uses some mol-
lifying ointment or plaister to it; but the wound
is still a wound, and in his opinion too; nor can
his cheerfulness cure it, or prevent his feeling the
anguish, tho' he regards it as little as may be, that
he may make his life as happy as it can be, man
is therefore not *a heap of contradictions* to himself, tho' men are to one another, but his mind
moves as regularly as other things; certain causes
have certain effects therein, and as the motives are,
and his passions are capable of being moved by
them, so his thoughts and actions are always naturally correspondent. Therefore, tho' love may
arise from an air, or a fancy, it cannot arise from
nothing; this is to burn without fire, or be moved
without a motive.

Nor does friendship, or any other quality or
thing thrive under any sort of necessity, but such
as is agreeable to its own nature. Constraint can
neither procure friendship, nor preserve it. Friendship I take to be a settled love, arising from a harmony of tempers and agreeable conduct; now
what constraint of any foreign nature can be be-
neficial to this? Two persons living together, so
as in time to become intimately acquainted with
one another, may be a means to friendship; but
if they know each other, and find no disposition
to it, forcing them to dwell together will not procure it. Persons already jaded with each other's
conversation, have but little lust to friendship by
being forced to live together; therefore, even on
this score, confinement can do no good. Nature
chuses rather to seek a help near at hand, than far
off; and therefore makes the most it can of what
it has opportunity of doing, and that is all that's

in it, but confinement to enjoyment, damps the sense and feeling of it, and contracts a honey-sun to a honey-moon. This way therefore of drawing the marriage-knot close, strains and often breaks it. Friendship, where it is solid and sincere, undoubtedly gains by friends living together; but such never chuse to part. Where 'tis wavering and uncertain, it may as well go as stay, since 'tis a thing indifferent, and being so, there's no damage done, whether it does the one or the other; but a load of hateful constraint lying upon it, is more likely to crush it to death, than to wedge it into the parties who feel the uneasiness of the load that oppresses them.

People of *common prudence* will act as common prudence directs them in all common affairs, but prudent or not they must be under one common confinement, and from this is expected to arise a common good! The same argument will as well prove that, in a kingdom where the subjects are made slaves by superior power, and impoverish'd by the authority of law, their rebellious tempers will subside, and they will become easy in thraldom, which otherwise would enflame into the most deadly rebellion, were they inraged or under the prospect of an easy success. Therefore slavery is rather to be chosen than liberty, as the more happy state

If the common consequence of marriage be only a *honey-moon*, followed with a number of *years under coldness, disdain and difficulties*, none but fools would marry, all persons of common prudence would dread the drawing that knot close, which ties a month's delight to an age of disquietudes and mourning. Love is doubtless a *restless and impatient passion*, when unsatisfied; but, if satisfied, does it prove the same also? Our passions will be restless and impatient to dissolve ~~the bands of~~ such love, **bands** as as the destroyer of its rest : For the God of love labours fix days to enjoy his fabbath on the seventh.

Obj In the third place (*says my author*) we must consider, that nothing is more dangerous, than to unite two persons so close in all their interests and concerns, as man and wife, without rendering the union entire and total. The least possibility of a separate interest must be the source of endless quarrels and jealousies. What Dr. *Parnel* calls *the little pilfering temper of a wife*, will be doubly ruinous; and the husband's selfishness being accompanied with more power, may be still more dangerous.

A. Where can the danger be to any one of having power to relieve one's self from misfortunes when they come? Whatever evil may accidentally arise from it, I believe it is what every one had rather chuse, than lie at the mercy of another's power, which is what all mankind dread. As this scheme is as good for one party or sex as the other, so none can dislike it with prudence, or disapprove it with reason. If a man does not conceive it dangerous to himself, to disunite one that is, or rather ought to be closely united to his interests, and unite another that he has reason to believe will be so, who is to judge for him? Every man should know his own interest best; and what makes it necessary for him to part with his wife. Quarrels and jealousies, separate interests and a pilfering temper, are some of the things complained of, that a divorce, or even the fear of a divorce may remedy.

Obj. Should these reasons against voluntary divorces be esteemed insufficient, I hope nobody will pretend to refuse the testimony of experience. At the time that divorces were most frequent among the *Romans*, marriages were most rare; and

K *Augustus*

Augustus was obliged by penal laws to force the men of fashion in *Rome* into the married state.

A. The gentleman answers himself——" A cir-
" cumstance which is scarce to be found in any o-
" ther age or nation ;"——and therefore not the natural consequence of the liberty of divorce. But does experience tell us, that we live happier in a married state, than those have done and do where this liberty has been and is allowed ? Could the enquiry and comparison be made, it would no doubt confirm the argument in favour of liberty.

It remains then, that those who intend to enter into a social state in expectation of felicity, should take care not to plunge themselves into such a one, as becoming unhappy, is incurable ; nor be drawn by bad customs into bad consequences ; nor be deluded into a state of real sorrow, irremediable, to avoid an imaginary state of sin : But be assured, that honest minds cannot sin ; and what does not injure others, men have or ought to have nothing to do with.   At all times indeed a prudential conduct is necessary, and a good character is valuable ; yet a conformity to some customs to preserve the latter, is sometimes the occasion of its being sacrificed, experience has told me so.   Tho' a good name is better than life, in vain we expect to preserve it in misery from infamy, be it thrown upon us ever so undeservedly.   Avoiding the means of irretrievable misfortune, is the best means to avoid the slander of the multitude, which is generally rash and wrong.

Since it is confessed, that without the liberty of divorce, *it is not good for a man to marry*, tho' it is declared, that *it is not good for a man to be alone* ; then it is good for a man not to give up the liberty he naturally has, to stand the very unequal chance of being miserable without redemption, to prevent
him

him from committing adultery. Tho' mifery is only faid to be the effect of fin, yet in this cafe men and women are made miferable, to prevent them from finning, like whipping a boy to prevent him from robbing an orchard; which he either has no difpofition of doing, or whipping him prompts him to do. I cannot think it is a man's duty to run the hazard of being miferable, if he can prevent it; therefore I cannot think it a man's duty to bring it on himfelf by matrimony, or mutilate himfelf to avoid it; yet, in my opinion, an honeft and conftant nature finds the moft real and durable happinefs.

The fociety of chofen mates by mutual agreement, is preferable to any other ftate, as natural honefty is to that of honefty by conftraint. Ti l the liberty of divorce is granted by law, if you are in a ftate of life which enables you to bear the charge of a family, where's the crime to take the woman you love upon fuch conditions as you both agree to. If both agree to meet or part, what has the law to do with it? The ceremony may join and often has join'd thofe not fit to be join'd, whom neither God nor nature joins. The form of marriage may be, where the fpirit is not; but fuch are *dead works*: 'Tis like *the dead burying their dead, or the form of godlinefs without the power of it, from which* we are commanded to *turn away.* Where the fpirit of love and fincerity is, there is truer marriage without the form, than the form without the fpirit; the one are alive to enjoyment, the other dead to it while they live. But thofe that nature joins in conftant affection, God joins; and whether with form or without, no man ought to feparate them. Tho' thefe are man and wife with the form or without, yet better without, that no evil reftraint be laid on good nature, but what the nature of things makes neceffary, that man's

meddling

meddling fpoil not God's joining : For if God, or
love, forfake thofe that are gone aftray from him,
and an evil fpirit from the Lord feize the man or
woman, as it did king *Saul*; fo that their nature
now chang'd, alters their condition from felicity
to infelicity, from good to evil, let the bands of
evil be broken , for living together in fin, is living in adultery, or worfe . For now only force
joins them, and fometimes luft, not love. If luft
be the only joining caufe, they are no more one
flefh, than a man and his harlot is, who are joined
by the fame caufe; and when the caufe is the fame,
the confequence will be the fame. Therefore thefe
ought to part, and feek elfewhere in a feparate ftate
the blefling that both being together cannot poffefs
and enjoy.

That man and woman were made for the enjoyment of each other, in fuitable circumftauces,
the reafon and fitnefs of things fenfibly difcover ;
but not any man for any woman, is alfo plain ; becaufe if all were equal, there could be no choice
of one, nor exception againft another, none could
be particularly affected or difaffected with one
more than with another ; and then all muft be
made alike both in body and mind : But feeing
there is infinite variety,'there are infinite caufes of
concord and difcord in the general nature of the
human kind and fex ; therefore love teaches a man
to diftinguifh one from many, and to know the
pleafure of fixing his affections on a fingle object,
which he that does on one worthy to be beloved,
enjoys in her the delights of the whole fex.

Happinefs is found to take up its abode only
with thofe, whofe agreeable difpofitions, regularity
of conduct, conftancy of temper, and ability of
circumftances are fitly prepared for its reception
and entertainment ; which is expected, but rarely
found, in an only death-diffolving married ftate.

The

The essence of matrimony lies in the end, *viz.* the good of society and care of posterity, not in the means that are ill adapted thereto. 'Tis the good intent of the action well conducted to its end that sanctifies it. Those laws of man that generally produce misery or infelicity, are not the laws of equity, which ought to be understood in every covenant or contract, even tho' the terms are not expressed.

If two persons are married according to law, however unequal their fortunes or rank in life were before marriage, it throws them so much on a level, that all gratitude soon vanishes from the meaner, whose circumstances are raised thereby, tho' obliged as much as one person can oblige another, for generally the needy party treats the other with ingratitude and indignity for the favour received, tho' it was all that one could desire, or the other give. I cannot conceive that marriage ought to annul the laws of gratitude. Ingratitude on either side must needs be productive of misery. But if ever so miserable, the law affords them no mercy; 'tis best therefore for a person to have the power in his or her own hands, by not formally doing what can never be undone. This is as good for the woman, as the man. Many a man spends a woman's fortune lavishly and in debauchery too, only because the law gives him possession, and it is not in the wife's power to restrain him. I was acquainted with a youth, a seeming Saint, who had no substance, that by the solicitation of his relations got the favour of a young widow of three thousand pounds fortune, and not long after he was possessed of her and all her effects, which she generously yielded to him, took to drinking, gaming and whoring, till he soon brought himself and the young gentlewoman to poverty; from which she had the good fortune to be removed by death.

Without

Without the ceremony, both parties poffefs their own fortune. A woman's property, unlefs fhe give it away by marriage, is her own; her man has a right to fpend no more of it than fhe pleafes; but when married, fhe muft fpend no more than he pleafes. Suppofe a man and woman, after fome time living together, find reafon to part, which they may do when the power is in their own hands, not having parted with their natural right by ceremonious complaifancy; what is the woman afterwards worfe than a widow? If fhe is in good circumftances, fhe may more eafily procure for herfelf a man to her liking, than a poor widow, and more eafily too preferve her fubftance and her perfon from ruin and ill ufage, than if fhe gave the man all fhe had by ceremonious condefcenfion, for fear fhe fhould be guilty of living in adultery. I knew a man and woman who cohabited together, and were thought to be legally married. The fubftance with which they traded, was the woman's, the man proved extravagant, and of ill conduct in bufinefs; fo that they were in a fair way to ruin, when neceffity obliged the woman to declare herfelf unmarried: She turn'd off her man, and fav'd the remainder of her fubftance, with which fhe carried on bufinefs with fuccefs, and foon after got another mate, who is a prudent man, and whether married or no they live happily together. A woman's dependence upon what is her own when it is fufficient, is better than a dependence on the precarious pleafure of a man who is a fanctified hufband, and for that reafon may if he pleafes be a fanctified villain. Many are the cafes which fhew the parties had better cohabit unbound, that the party aggrieved may be able to redrefs the condition by a feparation, than fubmit to a condition that admits of no redrefs. Nature teaches us that an unconfcionable yoke, which cannot

not

not be rectified by law, should be redressed by pre-vention. If law forbids the cancelling of cruel bonds, nature directs us not to sign and seal them. Marriage, as it now is, is entring into obligations to do or bear, what is oft impossible to be done or born by the contracting parties on one side, and sometimes on both sides. However the necessity of circumstances may bind, nature will still be the same. *Naturam expellas furca licet, usque recurret.*

Therefore we are not to take our standard rule of conduct from arbitrary precepts or practice, that receive their sanction from opinion, authority or custom ; for the most rational part of mankind are now generally agreed, that the reason and fit-ness of things is the fundamental rule of right, by which all human judgment, law and conduct should be directed.

'Tis not wisdom to barter away freedom, at least without an equal compensation (if an equal can be) and a reasonable happy prospect. Where great love or great interest tempts, let those that please try their fortune : As to others, that have no such temptations to bondage, in my opinion, nei-ther the ceremony, nor the parson performing it combines the heart or sanctifies the action, of those that sacrifice themselves at the altar.

When the ties of reputation in a married wo-man lose their hold, and the sense of forbidden pleasure drowns the sense of guilt, the ties of con-science have no force ; and in such case, how can a poor husband insulted with cuckoldom find re-dress. 'Tis a crime for him to be jealous, for tho' the circumstances are strong, nothing can justify his jealousy but the proof of the fact, which may more easily be a thousand times committed, than once proved. And even then, O cruel bonds ! they cannot be so easily cancell'd as made ; whereas the cord ought to be as easy to untie, as to tie ;

and

and in the fame manner, for which an honeſt man
would not grudge the parſon even double fees,
and alſo adore him as his redeemer, if he did not
his maſter as ſuch. Then indeed the Church
would have the power of binding and looſing; but
becauſe the parſons only ſhut, and no man can
open, they lie open to the contempt of all men;
for all men hate and deſpiſe thoſe that bring them
into miſery, but can do nothing to help them out
of it. Now, if the married part, (for the gates of
hell cannot confine ſome together, tho' in the devil's hour the powers of darkneſs join'd them) the
huſband muſt allow a maintenance or ſomething
towards it, to her that he has no longer any thing
to do with, (tho' I would have him put her away
in rather better than worſe circumſtances he took
her in, if poſſible) ſhe don't deſire to diſſolve the
marriage bonds, having the liberty of jilting at
pleaſure, and the ſatisfaction at the ſame time of
keeping her cuckold in confinement, by preventing
his happineſs with a better mate. I wiſh this be
not one cauſe why women are generally againſt
divorce, or I know not why they ſhould oppoſe it;
for ſet the bad conſequences of both ſtates, married
and unmarried againſt each other, and thoſe that
have not bartered away their freedom will find the
benefit of it. Certainly 'tis as much the advantage of
a good woman to be delivered from the tyranny and
ill uſage of a bad man, as for a good man to be
freed from the torments of a bad woman; unleſs
it is becauſe the female party are conſcious, that
'tis eaſier for them to captivate men, than keep
them; and if ſo, their charming qualities are more
ſuperficial than real; they pleaſe the fancy, but
will not ſtand the proof. But men, ſay they, are
fickle and inconſtant creatures, ever roving and delighted with novelty; ſuppoſing this, are not women the ſame? What pleaſure then can they take
in

in confinement more than men? But the truth is, all are not fo of *either* fex, tho' fuch are fome of *both*. So volatile and inconftant a humour cannot be bound; confequently cannot make a good hufband or wife; and it is not defirable to be confin'd to a bad one.

" If the divorce be with the woman's confent, " what has the Law to do with it; if without her " confent, it is either *juft*, and fo ought to be, or *un-* " *juft*, and to be divorc'd from an unjuft man can be " no injury : But fuppofe it is, and the law returns " her back to him from whom fhe was *expelled*, or " *intreated* to be gone, and fhe lives apart, a *mar-* " *ried widow*; is not this a miferable redrefs? *But* " *the man is tired of his old, and wants to have a new* " *wife.* If he be tired let him go. It muft be a " much wifh'd-for life, for a woman to live with " a hufband that is tired of her! *The man's inconftant,* " *and delights in change.* An inconftant lover is not " worth keeping, much lefs is an unconftant " hufband.

Let us look into the cuftom of other Countries, Divorce is allowed and practis'd by moft nations in the world, except the chriftians, and even by fome of them, particularly thofe of the *Greek* Church. And generally all others that join one woman to one man only, permit an eafy manner of divorce to thofe that prove falfe to their conjugal duty, and in cafes of great offence or diftate.

As to the indiffoluble ceremonious noofe, " In " *Sicily* after the Articles of marriage are fign'd by " the contracting parties, the bridegroom may con- " verfe freely with his bride, and fometimes they " cohabit many years together without the office of " the Church. Some of the *Hollanders* have alfo " feveral children before they pafs through thofe " formalities; and defer that affair till near their " death; and the children fo born are efteemed

L   " and

" and inherit as *legitimate*. So that (*says the wag-*
" *gish author of marriage ceremonies*) the benefaction
" of the priestly function, is not thought indispen-
" sibly necessary to the making such a commerce
" not criminal, though in other places, they have
" wheedled mankind into such a belief."

I contend not for the liberty of men's having more
wives than one, or of having *concubines*, which I
take to be *mistresses to wedded men*, for such they appear in the Scripture to be; but for the free enjoyment of virtuous love, and for the free dissolution
of it when it is otherwise.

" *When fix'd to one, love safe at anchor rides,*
" *And braves the fury of the wind and tides;*
" *But losing once that hold, to the wide ocean borne,*
" *It drives away at will, to every wave a scorn.*"

Love is true no longer than it is free; she can
only be bound with her own girdle. No violence
can force, nor fetters bind her. She forces without
violence, and binds without fetters.

———— " *No Law is made for love;*
" *Law is to things which to free choice relate,*
" *Love is not in our choice, but in our fate.*"

But because all are not bad, 'tis probable these
precautions will have but little effect, men and women will run all hazards in hopes of prizes, tho' ten
to one are blanks.

" *But yet if some are bad, 'tis wisdom to beware;*
" *And better shun the bait than struggle in the*
" *snare.*"

Not that a man is to expect his wife or consort
to be a *faultless creature*, such as he fancies
angels are; but he should consider her as human nature with himself, not without some
failings; and if they are such as can be
borne with, they ought to be borne with. It
conduces much to man's happiness, and shews

a noble nature, to bear with what is tolerable. If there be an affection and endeavour to pleafe, that good difpofition is fanctity. As long as one can engage the other's affections (which it is their mutual interefts to do, who live together) both are fecure and happy; and when that fails to be done in a married ftate, whatever fecurity the woman may imagine her ftate to be, fhe is fecurely miferable; for two perfons to be enabled or obliged to live together in fpite of each other, is uncomfortable living: But this is eafy to be prevented, by entring into fuch contracts only as the contractors may be able to perform: Confider, what does marriage do, but lay an obligation to keep a covenant without giving nature any ability to do it. 'Tis like the confecration of Prieftcraft, which pretends to put holinefs into earth and ftones, that never had any, nor ever can have. It calls marriage holy, but adds no holinefs to it, like that of making holy water for baptizing a child, which only wets the infant, but neither makes the water nor the child holier than before. It gives not the leaft ability to love or honefty, and yet binds to the practice of both: But love and honefty are the offspring of nature and liberty, not of art and confinement; thofe that have them not in a ftate of freedom, will not have them in a ftate of bondage, no more than fuch as neceffity produces, the appearance without the reality, the dead carcafe without the living foul. Love or affection are the foul of enjoyment, without this, all is unfavoury and unfatisfactory.

Wedlock, which is a lock indeed, opened to let the unwary in, and in which ftate the wifeft and ftrongeft men find no opening but in death to get out, feems to be fo ordained to difcourage marriage entirely by thofe religious phlegmatic drones, who thought a fingle life a fanctified, and

L 2 marriage

marriage an unfanctified ftate, at beft rather to be tolerated than encouraged, as we read 1 *Cor.* vii. *It i good for a man not to touch a woman; never-theless, to avoid fornication, let every man have his own wife, and every woman her own hufband* It feems to me by thefe words, as if it was good for married perfons not to touch one another, only to avoid fornication they were permitted; as if it was an unholy thing to make ufe of the fenfe of feeling: And 'tis likely many parfons if they had not a carnal feeling themfelves, or could fubdue it more than others, would condemn it ftill, for they have but little knowledge of human nature The fame A-poftolic batchelor gives his judgment thus · *To the unmarried and widows, I fay, it is good for them if they abide even as I. But if they cannot contain, let them marry; for it is better to marry, than to burn.* But, like other men, he was not always in one mood as to thefe things. At another time, he advifes *the hufband to give to the wife all due benevolence;* but that might be when he was either in a more fanguine mood, or after his married female difciples had complained of the want of carnal love in their believing hufbands, and *murmur'd that they* laid *neglected in the* nightly *ad-miniftration*

A man and woman who behave lovingly and ho-neftly to each other, can never accufe themfelves of either fornication or adultery, it is juft and in-nocent in the nature of the thing to any reafonable confcience, they may very well anfwer it to the fpi-ritual court within their own pure and uncorrupted minds and judgments; but if their confcience be governed and directed by another fpiritual court, whofe partial judgment is directed by intereft, they will judge it to be as they are directed to judge, which will certainly be what fuits the inter-eft of fuch court to make it But if honefty of

heart

heart and pure affection be the motive to good actions, and our rule to judge of them, then all natural impulses conducted by such motives, are pure, good, right, and fit to be done; nor is there any evil in such actions, whatever may be the unforeseen consequence, or the censorious judgment of stupid ignorance and perverse prejudice; and who can help people's wrong notions of things. They that don't go to church are deem'd Schismatics, and those that don't believe as the church believes are called Heretics, but what are any of them the worse for that, since honesty is not limited to orthodoxy. True courage, which a right conscience helps to procure, is requisite to dash impudence. How in the nature of things can that man and woman be adulterers, that are constant and honest to themselves? Or how can their children be bastards, who are the offspring of a faithful couple? There are many married whores and whoremongers, and many bastards are born in wedlock.

If the end of marriage be answered, *viz.* the benefit of society and posterity, where's the piety in contending for a superstitious ceremony? And where's the virtue of it, when a sham or scoundrel parson at the *Fleet* shall so bind the holy noose, that the greatest unholiness cannot dissolve it. If this agree with national piety, what sort of piety is that which such impious wretches have performed to the ruin of thousands, without any redress? Certainly the Apostles said right, *If the case be thus between a man and his wife, it is not good for a man to marry.* But the case was well enough, before it was made bad by adulterous sentiments of divorce.

I am persuaded if the liberty of divorces were granted by act of parliament at reasonable rates,

fees

fees or fines diſcreetly manag'd and well apply'd,
it might in time bring in ſufficient to diſcharge
the debts of the nation : But as the government
has given to prieſts the benefits of marriage, and
permitted them to marry, without which all married people would be in an unſanctify'd ſtate : So
I willingly acquieſce, if the ſuperior powers pleaſe
to give parſons the benefits of divorces, not doubt-
ing but then they would plead as heartily for that
liberty as I have done.

Sect. III.
Of Public Whoring.

GOOD and Evil are known by the *nature* and *consequence* of actions ; in the distinguishing which, we are to use reason in governing our appetites, affections and passions ; not in mortifying or crucifying them (as the notion of some is) but conducting them in a proper channel. *Appetites, affections* and *passions* are the springs of life, to exterminate them is to destroy all the good that life can be productive of, and even life itself. To *regulate* these, and to direct men so to act, as to prevent bad consequences to themselves, and others, as much as can possibly be avoided, is as much as is necessary. To be able to do this, 'tis proper to consider and define, what moral good and evil is : This can be determined only by a judgment form'd on the nature of things, not directed by arbitrary laws or precarious accidents

Human good and evil, respects human creatures only, and depend on their *circumstances.* No moral law is absolutely good or evil in all variety of cases, for as the case or circumstance varies, so the good or evil of the action will vary with it, We may not *kill*, to do it unlawfully is *murder ;* but to kill a criminal, or an enemy in war, is *lawful.* 'Tis not a crime to eat and drink, unless we do it to excess, and so hurt ourselves, or devour the property of others, and so do hurt to others Moral good and evil being limited to the nature of man, it must needs be, that actions which are injurious

to

to none of the human species, and neceffary to be done, becaufe the nature of man requires it, are not evil actions The *action* is not evil, which has not evil confequences, whatever the *evil* was that occafioned it. *By their fruits you fhall know them.* What does not injure man, cannot difpleafe God: For God governs man by laws, for the good of man: God himfelf is not benefited or injur'd by any thing that is in the power of man to do; becaufe from man, God receives nothing: From God, man receives all things.

Natural appetites that excite to the *propagation* and *prefervation* of human life, are not in their nature *evil* to man. *Copulation* is not an *evil* in its nature, but in fuch circumftances as are attended with inconveniency, and fome natural bad confequences in body or mind, as in thefe three particulars:

1. When there is a *natural unfitnefs in the bodily parts,* nature forbids to join together things unfit to be joined; for it is communicating pain and injury, inftead of pleafure and gratification. Yet perfons may be fo unnaturally bound together, by the *facred rites,* and fo difagreeably fitted for the enjoyment of each other.

2. When there is a *natural reluctance* of one party to comply with the difpofition of the other, 'tis a prohibition of nature. Whatever is done by one, contrary to the will of the other, or not without *full confent* of both, marrs the felicity of enjoyment; and is attended with forrow and grief on one fide, as well as compunction and regret on the other, in a temper poffefs'd of *humanity.* Every thing contrary to true harmony is a violation of LOVE, and not its offspring. *Rapes* are of the moft brutal nature, and deferve fevereft punifhment. To force a virgin, fhould be efteemed

a crime equal to robbing a houſe. Forced marriages againſt the good will of both parties, is diſagreeable; it is an evil that produces laſting ſor-
row and unhappineſs; the yoking together adverſe
natures, nature forbids. There ſhould be a fitneſs
in body and mind to action, to make it fit and a-
greeable

3. By diſhonourable ſolicitation, fraudulent in-
ſinuation. and falſe promiſes, to debauch a mind
to an action, the natural conſequence of which is
injury and repentance, is alſo criminal. To de-
flour a virgin under pretence of marriage, and a-
bandon her, is a fraud and knavery, and is naturally productive of ill effects The intrinſic value of a maidenhead, tho' nothing in itſelf, is to
be eſteemed according to its current value in the
eſtimation of huſbands, and the conſequence of its
loſs to the young woman's future felicity, and perhaps not hers alone. This makes it evil, enhances
the crime, and ſhews the iniquity of the fraud;
which might be leſs fatal, if divorces were allow'd:
For it would not then be productive of ſuch evil
conſequences. To tempt a virgin, or a virtuous
matron, to tranſgreſs the laws of chaſtity and con-
ſtancy, is not leſs a crime than defrauding one of
his property by artful and deceitful inſinuations;
as it tends to ſpoil the reputation and fortune of the
one in marriage, or if ſhe be afterwards married,
may render her leſs valued and beloved by her
huſband, and to diſengage the affections of the *tends*
other from her loving huſband: By debauching a
chaſte mind, ſhe is rendered leſs virtuous, and with
her huſband made leſs happy than before. Beſides,
'tis a robbery to the huſband in the higheſt degree,
to deprive him of what he moſtly values, *viz.* the
tender affections of his wife· When that is the
caſe, it is a loſs that can never be repaired. Sometimes to gratify one man's pleaſure, charge is

M   brought

brought on another, which the actor would be very much offenced, was he in the husband's case, to be so used. This is doing by another, as a man would not willingly be done by, and is therefore a moral evil.

These things are evil, because of the injury committed, but the case is different where none are injured, and both parties are free, and pleased with each other's actions, and are under no engagements of restraint than their own nature and common prudence direct. I see no reason, why persons that are at their own disposal have not as much natural right to dispose of their own persons according to their own pleasure, as of their substance, income or estate, if the one be as much their property as the other. If it be not so, then people dare not for their souls sake say their bodies are their own, but if it be so, it is not evident why they ought to be punish'd for disposing of themselves as they please, especially when matrimony, as it now is, is often worse, or of more fatal consequence; nor will it ever be esteemed honourable by those that are unhappy, while the means of happiness are withheld

'Tis well known that in the satisfying every natural desire of man, especially those that give the most delight, nature needs a bridle not a spur; because more are injur'd by too great freedom than restraint. Therefore prudence steers the middle way, and therefore reason is given to regulate our desires, yet the moderate gratification of what nature makes necessary can be no crime, when the property of none is invaded, and none are injured by it. 'Tis only the immoderate use of pleasure, or seeking it to the detriment of others that makes it criminal; therefore this can be no reason to use a *muzzle* instead of a *bridle*, nor to make those

actions

actions criminal that are the incitements of innocent nature, which she alone ripens man for, and
conftrains his will to defire , and he cannot help
defiring what she fits him to enjoy, and which not
nature but cuftom makes criminal : For how can
they be culpable of committing evil to others, who
neither do nor intend any? And man or woman
cannot will evil to themfelves ; for evil confifts in
grief and pain The gratification of every fenfe
contributes to the pleafure of life or man's well-
being, and every fenfe was given to man for that
end, to be enjoyed within the bounds of reafon, in
proper circumftances, and thofe circumftances are
proper and reafonab'e, that are by joint confent,
and hurtful to none Pleafures enjoyed and com-
municated prudently within natural and reafonable
bounds, and with neceffary regard to health and
fubftance, fo as not to be attended with the appre-
henfion of guilt, or the fear of after-pain, are enjoyed with fatisfaction. What makes pleafure the
greater to an honeft mind, is to be fatisfied with
reafon how it may be enjoyed fo as not to difturb
the mind's felicity by felf-accufation or after-re-
flections : For the pleafures of fenfe are marr'd, if
the fruition is not with a full fatisfaction of mind,
which a good underftanding and a prudent conduct are always neceffary to promote.

As to eat to fatisfy hunger, makes not the action evil, for were it not for this, men would have
no defire to eat, nor find pleafure in eating, confequently could not eat at all ; fo the gratification
of carnal luft to the injury of none, is no evil, nor
is the luft or defire itfelf, for were it not for that,
(to which nature has join'd *love* to the obj ct to inforce it) all procreation and the pleafures and vir-
tues of a focial life and family relations would be
at an end . Therefore, barely *to look on a woman
to luft after her,* without fome other explanatory

words,

words, *is not committing adultery in heart* : 'Tis not
an evil, becaufe unavoidable, and fometimes neceffary. If carnal luft be in itfelf an evil motive, it
muft be fo at all times, or in all cafes, and confequently is fo in a married ftate ; for in this cafe
marriage don't change the motive to the action ; if
it did, it would either be not done at all, or be very
ill done. It is not evil to gratify the natural lufts
of fenfe, by which life and being are fupported
and propagated, but to do it to the prejudice of
others. Where neither party injure each other,
but a man's natural appetite is fatisfy'd by the ufe
of an obliging courtezan, if he is under no legal
ties to another that ought in reafon to reftrain him,
but pleafure is mutually given and received, I
cannot fee any evil to be in the action more than
in the defire ; which defires being infus'd by nature for the good of man, vigorous in the beft, and
unavoidable in all in whom they are, which man's
will or wifdom cannot prevent, are not evil, tho'
thro' the mift of falfe divinity they be made to
appear, and be accounted fo. 'Tis the forbidding
it, makes it criminal, or rather to be efteemed as
fuch : For this defire does not arife from a vicious and corrupted mind, but is the genuine off-
fpring of pure nature in the pureft minds. The
defire of mutual enjoyment is natural to maturity,
health, and an uncorrupted and vigorous conftitution. Are men to crucify thefe common difpofitions given them of God as temptations to evil,
which invite them to participate of the fatisfaction
their nature requires, and circumftances afford ;
which are the moft diftant from ill nature of any
defire in man, when guarded from all injurious in-
tentions ?

He that cannot refrain, let him marry, is the precept : But there are many precepts from the fame
authority, that have wanted much amendment in
practice. When precepts of virtue are ftrained

too high, they are either impracticable or become vicious in their confequences. All men who cannot refrain, are not proper fubjects of matrimony. If fuch marry as are unable to provide for their offspring, they make themfelves and their offspring miferable. To fay another may refrain becaufe I can, or think I can, is to meafure every man's nature by my own, or by my own imaginations; which is certainly the effect of ignorance, and has been the caufe of impracticable laws and fevereft cenfures; not lefs ftupid than to fuppofe all mankind can believe one and the fame inevi 'ent propofition that is propos'd to them. The natures of men are fo very different, that what one man can do, another cannot; and he muft be very ignorant of human nature, who does not know that every different man has a different ability The not duly regarding this, occafions erroneous opinions of good and evil, bad laws and government. If every man and woman cannot refrain who are not in proper circumftances of marrying, then fome indulgence for thefe fhould be found out and granted

If perfons in a condition of life incapable to bring up their offspring, were affifted by the public in bringing them up, this objection would be removed. When inability in wealth is the only unqualifying circumftance, to help and affift their wants by public charity, is a public good, 'tis giving proper encouragement, and doing juft honour to matrimony To fuccour the children of unfortunate parents, when born in or out of wedlock, is certainly a public good to children, as well as to their parents, who are afraid or afhamed to own them. Since no age of the world could prevent an unfortunate offspring, the beft thing that appears at prefent neceffary to remedy this, is to give fuch encouragement to the Foundling Hofpital,

tal, as may enable them to bring up the infants sent thither for the service of the public, which may be a means to save the lives of thousands: Or, overseers of the poor should be obliged to take care of all such children as are sent them, without enquiring after or punishing the mothers of them for not being able to maintain them This sort of charity should be supported by the batchelors and widowers of *Great-Britain* who have no children, that those who do not marry for fear of charges, may have the less objection against it on that account. This is taking a necessary care of posterity, and rendering them useful to society.

They that cannot contain, are directed to marry, because *'tis better to marry than to burn*. But what if by their nature and circumstances, it is not proper for them to marry, and yet they cannot help burning ; nor, if married, will the burning cease, for tho' some can contain themselves without marrying, others cannot with. Those that marry should have dispositions peculiarly fitted for that state, these make it honourable indeed ; those that have not, make it dishonourable and unhappy. As persons are differently disposed by nature, which can never be eradicated, they will pursue different ways, and different sorts of happiness 'Tis contrary to nature and the design of providence, that all should be regulated by one method, they can no more be brought to one practice, than they can all embrace the same articles of faith. Certain it is, that there are some dispositions which cannot refrain, and as certain I think it is, that there are some th ought not to marry, not only those who are not in circumstances of taking care of a family, but also such whose natures are not suited to that state As 1ft, the intemperate, whose libidinous nature one to one is not sufficient to satisfy , nor, 2dly, those turbulent tempers who can

neither

neither long enjoy peace themfelves, nor fuffer
peace to be long enjoy'd where they are   3dly,
Perf : s of unftable temper are not fit to be married , the inconftant being never pleafed with any
thing long, cannot be long happy, nor make their
mates fo   4thly. And perfons without natural affection are not proper fubjects of matrimony;
where this is wanting, the natural duties incum-
bent on married folk to perform towards each o-
ther, can not be difcharged. Such tempers are
the caufe of much infelicity in wedlock. If an
office be required of perfons unqualified for the
performance of it, 'tis an unfit undertaking , fuch
ought either not to be put into that office, or being in it, to be difcharged from it, or at liberty
to leave it.   Therefore that fome are not fitly
qualified to marry, yet by nature are ripe for enjoyment, needs, I fuppofe, no further proof Tho'
the reftraining this luft is not deftructive of our
own exiftence, as not eating and drinking is , yet
becaufe it is deftructive of the exiftence of pofterity, the defire of fatisfying the inclination of the
former is not lefs ftrong than the defire of fatisfying that of the latter, in moft conftitutions. So
very ftimulating is the itch of coition, that men
and women run all hazards to enjoy what nature
vigoroufly prompts them to ; fo that neither the
fears of fhame, nor difgrace, penance, punifhment, fines, poverty nor death, nor yet the belief
of eternal damnation, can prevent even the righteous, as well as the profane, from this pleafing
trangreffion. So that no laws nor combinations
of men for reforming others (made mad by abfurd
notions of religion) have ever been able to put a
ftop to it ; becaufe it has its root in the ftrength
and perfection of the human conftitution and ani-
mal life ; therefore 'tis impoffible to root it out. or

to

to prevent thofe effects which have their caufe in nature.

Many actions are not evil in the nature of things, which are evil by the laws of every country, and the reafon is, becaufe no country makes the nature of things the univerfal ftandard of law, as they ought to do ; and they do it not, becaufe it fuits the interefts of thofe that have an influence in making thofe laws, to act contrary to nature's laws or the dictates of pure nature : Or elfe it is owing to the ignorance of the legiftators, in not rightly underftanding the exigency of things and human nature When this is the cafe, and injurious laws are eftablifhed, the impofition or iniquity becomes fafhionable, and gives it a fanction ; and then he that breaks fuch arbitrary laws, fhall be deemed as great a finner, as if he perverts the eternal laws of right and wrong, tho' it be in cafes where there is no fin, and which gives offence to none, but thofe whofe bigotry, ignorance or hypocritical virtue gives offence to human nature; enacting laws, which they cannot keep if they would, and which therefore they never do when a fecret agreeable temptation and private opportunity offers. Nay, for fear of having their actions made public, they debauch the virtuous. Thus, tinker-like, by endeavouring to ftop the leakinefs of human nature in one refpect, they make it greater in another, and render it more incurable. To fave their own reputations, they lay the foundation of private debauchery · For concealing nature does not alter it.

If any object, that the indulgence of public whoring will tend to the corrupting young men, this I think has little of argument in it ; for when their bodies are ripe for action, their minds are, and if nature has not vent one way it will find it by another. The moft modeft youths that debar themfelves of the natural means of difcharging the redundancy

dundancy which nature forms, find other means of doing it, called in thefe days *Onanifm*; a practice not fo natural, healthy or laudable, as that of fpending their rage on thofe who being free from diftemper are ready prepared to receive them, and to cool their courage. The indulgence therefore of public whoring well regulated, wil be found to be a public benefit, for when it is fuppref'd the private will prevail, and for that reifon private whores will be moft againft the permiffion of it; therefore all means taken by feverities totally to prevent it, makes it worfe. When a woman is once become a public whore, fhe has no expectation of getting a hufband, and yet has the fame defires towards man as honeft women that have hufbands; and woe to the man that marries a private whore What way can you punifh harlots that can reform them? If the difpofition be in nature, there is no way but depriving them of natural life. This will be as impolitic as drowning the world was for it heretofore (fuppofed by the judgment of facred writers to be done for that caufe); for as foon as the earth was delivered of its weight of water mankind grew, as foon as they could grow, as bad as before. Suppofe all the naughty people in this ifland were hanged or tranfported out of it this day, by to-morrow morning there wou'd be more, they would every day fprout like mufhrooms, while there was health and ftrength and human nature remaining If it was poffible it could come to a ftop here, people from other countries would come over; and thofe few honeft people that remained having no bold fpirited rogues to defend them, would be deftroyed for their fobriety, as they had deftroyed others for their wantonnefs, for God no more protects fools than finners. Carnal luft is an itch in young blood abounding with health and vigour, which

N

no remedies but such as sickness, old age and death can effectually cure. Marriage is prescribed as a remedy, but 'tis often but a palliative one, and the cure is frequently worse than the disease ; therefore young men are afraid to apply it, and married people when not pleased with their mates apply it in vain. Those that are single dread the remedy, and those that are married for the most part hate it ; because 'tis a remedy that allows of no remedy, it causes more mischief than it cures, and will do so as long as it is, *for better for worse till death parts.* This sort of marrying therefore gives cause to whoring ; for who had not rather do an evil they can repent of and mend, than do an evil they can never mend tho' they constantly repent of it ? The best cure for whoring, is to grant some reasonable liberty, that people upon trying and disliking may part as easily as they came together. Tho' this may not perhaps absolutely and effectually prevent whoring, yet it will be found to do it (I believe) the most effectually it can be done ; then there might be more reason to put penal laws in execution against it. And there would be good reason to do it, if proper husbands could be found for all the wanton women, and not only wives for poor fellows that want them, but their families taken care of who are scarce able to take care of themselves : Or, if parsons by preaching could change and restrain the exuberance of man's nature. Until these things are done, there is no proper cure for the malady complained of. But while God gives to men and women such strong and vigorous inclinations as they have, they will incline as they do one towards another. For as the powers of nature act mechanically on inanimate bodies, so do the powers of human nature (the passions, appetites or dispositions) actuate the human body, as opportunities or external circumstances permit or invite.

All

All actions should be regulated by reason in such sort as the nature of actions require. Give to natural use what nature requires: What is God or man benefited by any unnatural restraint? Or, how injured, when no injury is done to any one? But, methinks, I hear it objected, *Shall I take the members of* Christ, *and make them the members of an harlot? God forbid!* But sometimes harlots are the members of *Christ*; for he told the Pharisees, that such should *go into the kingdom of heaven before them*, for they believed in him, *Mat.* xxi. 31, 32. And as many a harlot therefore may be a member of *Christ*, who was a friend to publicans and sinners, in this case 'tis only joining one member of *Christ* to another, and they'll be equally sanctified. But if *he that is joined to the Lord is one spirit,* 1 *Cor.* vi. 17 then he that is joined to him is joined by a spiritual member; and if *he that is joined to a harlot is one flesh*, as the same Apostle intimates, that joining is by a carnal member, and so not by the same member by which he is join'd to *Christ*; consequently he does not take the members of *Christ* and make them the members of an harlot; but as *Christ* admonished, *Give to* Cæsar *the things that are* Cæsar's, *and to God the things that are God's*; so he gives to the spirit the things that are spiritual, and to the flesh the things that are fleshly. To each its proper member. St *Paul* seems to give the devil's things to the devil, 1 *Cor* v. when he orders them to give the *flesh* of the incestuous person to *Satan, that his soul might be saved*; meaning perhaps, Let him sow his wild oats, that his extravagant actions may bring him to repentance; perhaps, 'tis no great matter to us what he meant, but in particular it seems to be giving to Satan the things that are Satan's. It appears not to me to be any thing unnatural for a lover of *the son of man* to be a lover of *man*

The

The firſt council of the Apoſtles ordered the Gentile Chriſtians *to abſtain from eating blood, and things ſtrangled, from things offered to idols, and from fornication.* Theſe were injoined as ceremonious laws, and as ſuch the breaking any one of them is only breaking thro' a ceremony. If all are upon an equal foot, then fornication is no more criminal than eating a ſtrangled pullet or black pudding The difference ſeems only to be as the conſequences make it : For St *Paul* eſteems eating *things offered to idols* as no crime in itſelf, but in the conſequence that may ariſe from it by giving offence to a weak brother. So judge of other things then forbidden. There are actions lawful in the nature of things, that are not expedient.

He that cannot refrain let him marry, is not a fit precept to thoſe that are not in a condition to provide for a family , or are ſo far from being in a capacity to do it, that they are little able to take care of themſelves, unleſs public charity would take care of their children If this was done, many would be brought up that now periſh, and would in a great manner prevent whoring. I think it is no man's duty to enter into any contract, that he is not capable of performing Marriage or cohabitation is a ſtate that requires a ſettlement. He therefore that is not ſettled in the world, nor in a condition of ſettling himſelf, and marries or cohabits as a huſband with a woman, or ventures upon the getting children to maintain, does not well conſult the happineſs of himſelf, his partner, nor of poſterity, which it is ſo much the duty of all men to take care of, that he who does not or cannot do, muſt be ſtung with compunction and regret, if he is not inhuman. He cannot diſcharge that duty who is not in a condition to do it. Why ſhould any man enter into the ſtate he is not fit for? It is by this means there are ſo many poor,

and

and mankind in general so ill provided for Therefore to tolerate whores, and to take care of their children at the public charge, would be a public benefit, unless the public would take care of all poor people's children, the better to encourage marriage as was mentioned just now, and to prevent the fears of young men's entering into that state, allow of divorce for reasonable and just occasion, and make marrying and unmarrying to be performed in the same manner, and at the same expence.

If meddling with public women be thought a sin against posterity, by not promoting it; so is matrimony when ill, by ill promoting the good of posterity: For family contentions spoil the education of children, whereby their nature becomes evil, their manners deprav'd, and the morals of the nation corrupted as much as by any other means.

As for the *sin* of whoring, was it regulated so as not to be injurious to society, there would be none in it What is no injury to man can be none to God, whose laws are all calculated for the good of man; he himself being compleatly perfect, can receive no benefit or pleasure, nor any degree of injury or displeasure from human actions. For to suppose the contrary, either the one or the other, is to imagine that the pleasure of God or his happiness depends on the will and pleasure of man, or on his obedience or disobedience. And as to common women, no injury is done to them, by making use of them who are most fit for common use, their minds and bodies being already prostitute, and so qualified by their function, that preachers may spend their rhetoric, and logicians their arguments in vain, for the conversion of those that chuse that kind of life, their natures are addicted to. And he does no injury to himself by the use of them that receives none

from

from them, and only finds a difcharge neceffary for his health's fake. Therefore tolerating and regulating courtezans by proper authority would convert a private evil to a public good. The lefs violence and perfecution they are under, the lefs private difhonefty they will be guilty of, becaufe their neceffities will be the lefs ; for neceffity often makes people act contrary to their natural difpofitions, and corrupts thofe that might otherwife fhine in virtue. A woman, becaufe fhe is a harlot, is not therefore neceffarily a thief. 'Tis misfortune or neceffity that generally produces both. When whores find it their intereft to be honeft, they will be as honeft as others. Befides thofe, that are by nature fit for this public bufinefs, are not fit for wives; confequently, by indulging thefe, there will be the lefs number of bad wives. If they would behave well, fcarce any man will venture to take to wife one of thefe proftitutes; fo th t they who have begun it are under a neceffity of following on in the fame courfe. For thefe are thofe that either cannot contain, for if they could they would have done otherwife, or by other neceffity were reduced to it, and as long as the fame neceffity holds, the confequence will be the fame, unlefs a new neceffity of another kind arife to prevent it

'Tis certain that a proftitute is not a laudable employ, becaufe it is generally the effect of poverty ; but 'tis a tolerable one, becaufe better that than worfe ; 'tis an evil in human nature compared with the excellent union between one and one who dwell together in harmony ; but 'twill be found a neceffary evil, if rightly underftood, permitted and ufed. As great a fin as it is, poverty feems greater, for none but poor whores fuffer for their practice, therefore their fuffering is not the effect of their crime, but of their poverty · Therefore

diftreffing

diſtreſſing them more, cannot make them better; becauſe it increaſes their neceſſity, and makes the cauſe of proſtitution greater, and ſo reduces them to thieving, a worſe practice. 'Tis a neceſſary evil, becauſe the toleration of theſe is neceſſary to preſerve the chaſtity of others, and young men from everlaſting ruin by precipitate marriage which never can be remedied. Therefore it would be well, if in every town at leaſt ſo many as are ſufficient were permitted to abate the fire of thoſe that cannot contain, and yet may not be in proper condition to marry; and alſo to reduce to reaſon thoſe that are inclined to that ſort of folly or madneſs, and muſt have irreſiſtible vent. For nature ſupplies man with a plentiful ſtock of juice and ſpirits for pleaſure-ſake, more than can be waſted for procreation. And it is no injury to a man, when he comes to marry, to have enjoyed women with moderation before; the women themſelves being judges.

I wonder theſe women have never thought of another method of making themſelves or their profeſſion public, than that of patrolling the ſtreets, a very improper method which ſome think is too much in imitation of Satan, who is repreſented *walking about ſeeking whom he may devour*, that they have never thought of hanging ſomething ſcarlet out at the window of their lodgings, in imitation of their great patroneſs RAHAB, who hung out a ſcarlet line; it might be perhaps a rope covered with red cloth, *Joſhua* ii 18, 21. and who is afterwards numbered among the ſaints, *Hebrews* xi. 31. Or, if ſhe is a houſe-keeper, the ſign of *Mary Magdalene*, is not an improper one, whom holy church owns was a beautiful courtezan, and one of the moſt charming diſciples of the Lord *Jeſus*.

Public

Public whoring under proper regulations, is as neceſſary to a town, as a common place for evacuation is neceſſary to every houſe, without which all the houſe will ſoon be in a naſty pickle ; and ſome can as eaſily bear to have the fore-door of their houſe ſhut up as their back-door No violence or force can prevent a madneſs ſo natural to men and women Whatever reformers may think, they always make more miſchief by their violence, than they are able to prevent.

I conclude with a word of advice, firſt to young men. It is a hard matter to moſt to uſe moderation in the purſuit of pleaſure, whereby many are emaciated and die young: But 'tis the part of the prudent to follow a mean in all things. Extremes will either mar your underſtanding, or your manners. The flame that burns fiercely, the ſooner conſumes its fuel. Pleaſure is to be uſed only for the ſake of health and eaſe; which, becauſe it is hard to bridle within juſt bounds, I apprehend, that moſt wiſe men have required of you a total reſtraint. He that can wholly abſtain, keeps himſelf out of danger, and has ſafety inſtead of pleaſure, which often produces pain in its conſequences; and therefore requires care and conduct to regulate. 'Tis the greateſt prodigality to make a burnt-offering of yourſelves on *Venus's* altar A body drain'd of its juices, and macerated, makes a feeble old age. In all enjoyments 'tis good to beware of exceſs, and not be captivated with the love of pleaſure. It ſhould be made a refreſhment, not a toil; that after waſting your follies you may act the wiſer, that your minds may be more free for noble and neceſſary uſes. If you would enjoy mental pleaſures in old age, keep oil in your lamps to enlighten your upper rooms; therefore ſpend in moderation, and not too laviſhly. Purity of mind

ſhould

should be always preferved, that the corruption of pleafures do not corrode it. Fools only prodigally wafte their bodies, their health and their fubftance. 'Tis commendable to be always honeft and juft to woman, as well as to man, in the performing of contracts; that you do not by your own practice teach thofe difhonefty, that you have to do with. Let a confcientious care direct you. Never debauch any virgin, nor corrupt any matron, fince other more proper perfons may be enjoyed : Nor give any occafion to any to grieve by your falfhood, which muft give pain and regret to an honeft mind to have been the caufe of.

Let thofe that are in the *decline of age* be careful of the balfam of life, and not defire the return of youth, which they cannot obtain, nor too rigoroufly condemn thofe pleafures or follies they are not fo fitted to enjoy : But, content with what is paft, regard thofe more noble ficulties of reafon, the principal pleafure of the foul, when fenfitive pleafures begin to leave them.

To *virgins*. My greateft concern is for you; you muft endeavour to refift, with all your might, the temptations of young men, that would enfnare you; and take the utmoft care to truft none but fuch in whofe breaft lodges fentiments of virtuous honour, and who have a ftrict regard to truth, with whom you have a profpect of being happy all your days. You have the moft difficult part to act, and the only way to keep your fortrefs from furrendering is never to treat about it but when terms fit to be accepted are propofed by one whofe actions have been known not to give his lips the lye. Preferve your virginity for a hufband, that you may find the reward in his lafting love and good opinion of your chaftity and fidelity. Love and affection founded on virtue is the moft durable.

O   To

To *parents,* whose children by the force of youthful vigour and agreeable temptations have acted contrary to their wills : Consider what sensible and pleasing titulations you had yourselves when young, and forgive the faults that nature makes in those that have err'd. If you preserv'd yourselves in your youthful days, yet make some allowance for the difference of constitutions and circumstances. Which of you having children, had not much rather they make a slip that is recoverable as to condition, than be in a condition irrecoverably miserable Scarce any, with respect to their sons, but would chuse this ; and would as freely chuse the same, respecting their daughters, if they rightly considered things, and if the barbarous custom of making so wide a distinction where no such is, did not pervert the judgments of people, and occasion their partial censoriousness. This I mention to stir up in parents a placable forgiving nature, and to abate rash censure in all, not to corrupt any. What I have written, I intend for a general good ; and, I am disposed to hope, will be more conducive to it, than many writings that have a more sanctified appearance.

The SPEECH *of Mifs* POLLY BAKER, *faid to be delivered by her before a Court of Judicature in the Colony of* Connecticut *in* New-England ; *where fhe was profecuted the* fifth *time, for having a baftard child, which influenced the Court to difpenfe with her punifhment, and induced one of her Judges to marry her the next day* (a).

MAY it pleafe the honourable bench, to indulge me in a few words : I am a poor unhappy woman, who have no money to fee lawyers to plead for me, being hard put to it to get a tolerable living (b).

I fhall not trouble your Honours with long fpeeches, for I have not the prefumption to expect, that you may by any means be prevailed on to deviate in your fentence from the law in my favour (c).

O 2

(a) This ftory is attefted for truth, but whether true or no, the reafons that follow are true : but many perfons, in matters of belief, *ftrain at a gnat, and fwallow a camel* They cannot credit the truth of a ftory that has nothing improbable in it ; but can credit ftories reported by a credulous people to be done in diftant ages, and in a ftrange country, which are impoffible to nature

(b) No penny, no *pater nofter* whether in Law or Gofpel, the poor could feldom have right by law, and formerly 'twas *impoffible* for rich men to go to heaven by the gofpel, when *Chrift* and his minifters were poor, but if the cafe be the fame now, *Chrift* have mercy upon his minifters, for they are now rich.

vour (a). All I humbly hope is, that your Honours would charitably move the Governor's goodnefs on my behalf, that my fine may be remitted.

This is the fifth time, Gentlemen, that I have been dragged before your court on the fame account (d); twice I have paid heavy fines, and twice have been brought to public punifhment, for want of money to pay thofe fines (e). This may have been agreeable to the laws, and I don't difpute it; but fince laws are fometimes unreafonable in themfelves, and therefore repealed; and others bear too hard on the fubject in particular circumftances, and therefore there is left a power fomewhat to difpenfe with the execution of them (f), I take the liberty to fay, that I think this law, by which I am punifhed, is both unreafonable in itfelf, and particularly fevere with regard to me, who have always lived an inoffenfive life in the neighbourhood where I was born; and defy my enemies (if I have any) to fay I ever wrong'd man, woman or child   Abftracted from the law I cannot conceive (may it pleafe your Honours) what
the

(c) Religious finners have more affurance; they imagine, as they are taught Luke xviii that importunity will work upon their judge, and that therefore they fhall be heard for their much fpeaking, how much foever they fpeak againft it, or, why do they pray fo long, and often? Why fo often utter the fame expreffions over, and over again; if importunity be not the availing grace, if the beft prayer-monger or fpeech maker to God Almighty does not ftand the beft chance

(d) 'I was well they did not put her to death for being a witch, in getting five children without a hufband, which could certainly be done no way but by witchcraft

(e) If it was juft to inflict any punifhment or fine, it fhould have been inflicted on the man, the woman, I think, fuffered enough in bearing the children, and bringing them forth

(f) And very reafonable it fhould be fo, becaufe circumftances fo far alter the nature of things, that the fame action may be good or evil, as it is differently circumftanced.

the nature of my offence is *(g)*. I have brought
five fine children into the world at the rifque of
my life, and have maintained them well by my
own induftry, without burdening the townfhip *(h)*;
and would have done it better, if it had not been
for the heavy charges and fines I have paid *(i)*

Can it be a crime (in the nature of things I mean)
to add to the number of the King's fubjects in a
new country that really wants people? I own it,
I fhould think it praife-worthy, rather than a pu-
nifhable

(g) 'Twould be very hard by the laws of reafon and nature,
without the arbitrary authority of law, to prove her a criminal, or offender Can an inoffenfive life offend God, that does
not offend man?

(h) Surely the bringing them into the world, and bringing
them up, was fo much punifhment, that I believe few women
would do the fame to enjoy the tranfitory pleafure in getting
them, and as much as her trouble exceeded her pleafure, fo
much more than atonement fhe made for her fin, if that pleafure was fin, that fhe certainly did works of merit and fuper-
errogation And if her righteoufnefs more than balanced her
fin, certainly the fin was done away, and fhe ought to be
deem'd righteous, and the over-balance fhould be charged to
her credit in the book of life She ought not to be punifhed
for not having a father to her children, feeing fhe was both
father and mother to them

(i) Is not mulcting the poor parent for begetting children
out of the pale of matrimony, robbery, by the authority of
law, of the children's fupport To beget children is human,
or agreeable to the nature of man, but to deprive them of
their fubfiftence, or what ought to be theirs, is inhuman or
barbarous to human nature To enable parents to bring up
their children, is pious and charitable, but to difable them
from doing their duty by them, is impious and uncharitable •
And if the parents are poor, has a tendency to *murder* If
the confequence of fuch feverity reduce the parents to *fteal*, to
maintain themfelves and offspring, the fin is not in the parents,
but in the law, which lays them under that neceffity, for neceffity has no law, therefore cannot be faid to break any That
which makes the neceffity, makes the fin Wicked laws make
the people wicked And they that make thofe laws, are the
authors of all bad confequences fuch laws produce.

nifhable action (k). I have debauched no other
woman's hufband, nor enticed any youth: Thefe
things I never was charged with, nor has any one
the leaft caufe of complaint againft me, unlefs
perhaps the minifter, or juftice, becaufe I have had
children without being married, by which they
have miffed a wedding-fee (l). But can ever this
be a fault of mine? I appeal to your Honours.
You are pleafed to allow, I don't want fenfe; but
I fhould be ftupified to the laft degree, not to pre-
fer the honourable ftate of wedlock, to the condition I have lived in (m). I always was, and am
ftill willing to enter into it; and doubt not my
behaving well in it, having all the induftry, frugality, fertility, fkill and œconomy appertaining
to a good wife's character (n) I defy any perfon
to fay I ever refus'd an offer of that fort (o) On
the contrary, I readily confented to the only pro-
pofal of marriage that ever was made me, which
was when I was a virgin, but too eafily confiding
in the perfon's fincerity that made it, I unhappily
loft my own honour by trufting to his; for he got
me

(k) Which is moft praife-worthy, to get children, and take
care of them, or to get none and take care of none? Which
is moft conducive to the public good, or beft for the common-
wealth? Suppofing both to be good, yet which is the better?
Which is the more laudable, a private perfonal good, or the
propagation of public good? Frugality or hofpitality, where
either are practicable? Or, at leaft, if conftitution and circumftances require the one or the other, where is the crime of
practifing either?

(l) Becaufe both minifter and juftice marry there

(m) Undoubtedly it is better to be at a plentiful table,
and to live in credit, than to fnap at a bit now and then, as if
ore lived by ftealth, and be always betrayed

(n) Outfide goodnefs often carries off the prize, which,
thofe of modeft, hidden and intrinfic worth merit, but are
deprived of

(o) So that fhe was punifhed for her misfo-ture, not for her
fault

me with child, and then forfook me (*p*). That very perfon you all know; he is now become a magiftrate of this country; and I had hopes he would have appeared this day on the bench, and have endeavoured to mo 'erate the court in my favour; then I fhould have fcorn'd to have mention'd it, but I muft now complain of it, as unjuft and unequal, that my betrayer and undoer, the firft caufe of all my faults and mifcarriages, (if they muft be deem'd fuch) fhould be advanc'd to honour and power in the government, that punifhes my misfortunes with ftripes and infamy (*q*).

I fhall be told, 'tis like, that were there no act of affembly in the cafe, the precepts of religion are violated by my tranfgreffions (*r*). If mine then is

a

(*p*) 'Tis a moft fhameful thing, that men pretending to honour or confcience, fhould only pretend it to obtain their ends; which having obtained, they facrifice all honour and confcience, and yet would be thought to have it. But fo eagerly do moft men purfue pleafure and profit that they leave honour and confcience behind them in their amours and affairs, fo that few are to be trufted in thofe concerns.

(*q*) It muft be confefs'd, tho' 'tis difagreeable to be told, that people do not fuffer for their *crimes*, but for their *weaknefs, ignorance* and *poverty*; for if two perfons are guilty of the fame action (as in this cafe) he impotent and poor fuffer with fcandal, while the powerful and opulent generally efcape with impunity, and perhaps applaufe, tho' the poor may have neceffity to plead in their favour, and this is naturally the cafe, when actions that are not criminal in themfelves are fo made by law, contradictory in reafon and the nature of things, are by law or cuftom efteem'd juft. Sometimes indeed men fuffer for their riches, as when they fall into the hands of *high-way* robbers, or *high-church* robbers, as the inquifition in *Spain* and *Portugal*, where rich Hereticks are *murdered* by the law of that church, and the church by law too may *rob* them and their families of all their wealth, and this law is there deemed *holy* and *juft*.

(*r*) The precepts of any religion, which is not eftablifhed on the foundations of truth and *honefty*, (and they are generally founded on forms which are violated by truth and honefty.

a religious offence, leave it to religious punifhments. You have already excluded me from the
comforts of your Church communion : Is not that
fufficient? You believe I have offended heaven,
and muft fuffer eternal fire : Will not that be fufficient ? What need is there then of your addi-
tional fines and whipping (s)? I own, I do not
think as you do ; for if I thought what you call a
fin was really fuch, I could not prefumptuoufly
commit it. But how can it be believed that heaven is angry at my having children, when to the
little done by me towards it, God has been pleafed
to add his divine fkill and admirable workman-
fhip, in the formation of their bodies ; and crown'd
it, by furnifhing them with rational and immortal
fouls (t) ?

Forgive

nefty Religion, erected and eftablifhed on thefe, is good ;
and fuch religion only. All other is knavery, and tyranny,
and injurious to the natural rights of mankind , and aims to
make fovereigns, as well as fubjects its flaves and vaffals 'Tis
highly neceffary in every kingdom, that the king fhould be
head of the national church therein , or the church will be
his head If he keep not the church under his power, the
power of the church, that is, of the priefts, will keep the king
under The church will be always mild, when its power is
muzzled , and will do no hurt, when it cannot But every
church, when invested with power, will pour out the phials of
its wrath upon men

(s) If they believe eternal torments are the rewards of fin
in this life, when they teach others to believe, or that hereafter God will punifh all men according to their demerits,
what prefumption is it for them that believe fo, to take God's
work out of his hand (efpecially in fins faid to be againft him
only?) Or do they juftice now, in bringing his juftice on
themfelves by their own injuftice If this doctrine was really
true, and truly believed, I fee no need of punifhments here ;
all that need be done, is to convince men of the truth of it.
But men act, judge and punifh here, as if the truth of this
doctrine was very uncertain, not to be depended on , and very
little believed, tho' much talked of

(t) An evident demonftration, that the having baftard
children

Forgive me, Gentlemen, if I talk a little extra-
vagantly on thefe matters; I am no divine : But if
you, Gentlemen, muft be making laws, do not turn
natural and ufeful actions into crimes by your prohibitions (*u*)   But take into your wife confideration
the great and growing number of batchelors in this
country, many of whom from the mean fear of the
expences of a family, have never fincerely and ho-
nourably courted a woman in their lives, and by
their manner of living, leave unproduced (which is
little better than murder) hundreds of their pofterity
to the thoufandth generation.   Is not this a greater
offence againft the public good, than mine? Com-
pel them then by law, either to marriage, or to pay
double the fine of fornication every year (*x*)   What
muft poor young women do, whom cuftom has forbid to folicit the men ; and who cannot force themfelves upon hufbands, when the laws take no care
to provide them any ; and yet feverely punifh them,
if they do their duty without them ; the duty of
the firft and great command of nature, and of nature's God, INCREASE AND MULTIPLY ; a duty,
from the fteady performance of which, nothing has
been able to deter me ; but for its fake I have ha-
zarded the lofs of the public efteem, and have frequently endured public difgrace and punifhment ;
and therefore ought, in my humble opinion, inftead of a whipping, have a ftatue erected to my
memory (*y*).   P   *POST-*

children is no fin to God ; and the bringng them up, can be
no fin to man

(*u*) Actions *natural* and *ufeful* cannot be criminal in the reafon of things, tho' made to appear fo, by fuch prohibitions

(*x*) If marriage tend to the good of fociety, one might be
tempted to think, that a religion which difcourages it, was
given to men by God, as he was faid to have given *Saul*, a king
to the *Ifraelites*—in his anger.

(*y*) This fpeech is beyond all ftatues that can be erected to
eternize her memory, which demonftrate her to have been a woman of excellent SENSE, VIRTUE and HONOUR, maugre all
that may be faid to the contrary.

POSTCRIPT.

ALL that in the preceding pages may seem to reflect on *Jesus Christ*, for discouraging *divorce* and *marriage*, will be easily conceived to be no reflection on him, if he was *not* the Author of that discourse on this subject ; as I have all along, in honour of his *great* and *holy name* suppos'd: Which may be very well granted, if we consider, (1) That the first miracle he wrought, was at a marriage-feast, as 'tis alledged in favour of that ordinance. (2) That he declared, *he came not to destroy the law, but to fulfill it* ; that is, to enforce the doctrine and discipline of it ; but setting a law aside *destroys*, not *fulfills* it. (3.) That he *never blam'd* the woman of *Samaria* for having had five husbands, and then living with one that was *not her husband*. (4) That his gentle behaviour to the woman taken in the act of adultery, shews him to have been no severe Monk. (5.) That he very affectionately expressed his love to little children, *Suffer little children to come unto me, and forbid them not ; for of such is the kingdom of God*. (6.) That he encouraged *love* among his Disciples, which shews he would not have them live together in enmity (7) That his saying to the *Jews*, concerning *Moses, If ye believe not his writings, how will ye believe my words*, shew, that his words did not *contradict* the writings of *Moses*. If they did not harmonize, how is the belief of the one necessary to the belief of the other? If it be objected, that granting this *insinuation* to be *true*, that this discourse with the Pharisees had not *Christ* for its Author ; we shall be at a loss to know what he did say. I answer, better so, than say he *contradicted* himself, and *destroyed* the foundation he *built* on ; uttered things *absurd*, and delivered precepts *unnatural*. It is most becoming for Christians, to believe the *best* of him. If for these reasons, I may be excused

from

from intending to reflect on *Christ*, by consequence, excusing *me*, excuses *him*.

And my plea for tolerating *professed whores*, will be also found *pardonable*, if it be considered, that what is here proposed, is not against *Law* or *Gospel*; for the reasons for so doing, are offered with submission to the Law, to give them a *legal toleration*, and *regulate* their *practice*, that being managed with more *modesty*, *decency* and *decorum*, it may remove the present bad consequences attending it : Thus 'twill make the evil *less*, and of the *greater* evils before-mentioned, direct men to chuse the *least* : Nay, 'tis the best means that can be to prevent the shameful sin of *sodomy*. If 'tis objected, that this is encouraging *profaneness* and *impiety*; I answer, that cannot be ; for to *profane* any thing, is to use what is *holy* in an *unholy* manner ; but sure none will say, that the *things* I mean, which are better conceived than told, are like *Aaron's holy breeches*. And therefore their natural use, cannot profane what were not sanctified before

And as for the *impiety* of this toleration, I see none in it ; for who have been more pious than *public whores*? Who has *enriched* the *Church of Rome* more than they, and their lovers ? And what has more benefited *Protestant Churches*, than the *divorce* of King *Henry* VIII. Therefore this *carnal toleration*, and *indulging of divorces* will not be injurious to the *Gospel*; for these sinners generally frequent the Church as much as others, and make as pious an *Exit*, when they are not *persecuted*, which makes them *worse*, not *better*; and the *Gospel* always thrives best in a *soil fattened with sin*. Who are more generous, frank, open-hearted, open-handed, and charitable, than these ? And, if *Charity covers a multitude of sins*, sure it may cover this one. *Where sin abounds, grace does much more abound*; therefore sin is not injurious to Gospel grace.

What

What then, shall we sin, because Grace abounds? God forbid. *Where there is no law, there is no transgression.* Take away therefore the *law*, and you take away the *sin*; for 'tis none against *nature*, as has been shewn. These familiar social favours, which will always be wanted, sought for, and granted, both are and may be done, without prejudice to *society*. If they were permitted and regulated by *law*, they would then be *lawful*; a licence from the Commons, or County-sessions could do that. I don't think it would best answer the end proposed, to prevent private whoring, to stew them all up in one place or part of the town, rather to let them live where they will, and publish themselves by some feigned name, on the door or sign, as of *Helen, Flora, Dido, Cleopatra, Letitia, Constantia,* &c. But wherever they live, let them conform to the *laws,* that regulate their behaviour. Let none object, that this would be tolerating things *dishonourable.* Is not this world one of God's houses? And must not every house that is usefully furnished, have in it, what the Apostle calls, *vessels of honour and dishonour?* Are not chamber-pots necessary, as well as drinking-pots? All vessels can't be plates, tankards, and punch bowls. Do they that break the vessels for dishonourable uses, act wisely? The most despised things are of some use. *Our uncomly parts have more abundant comliness,* said the holy batchelor, which shews that he himself had been *pleased* with the *comly sight* of our *uncomly parts*; and they that prate against these *uncomly parts,* have them, and find them as necessary, tho' *hid,* as those parts that are deck'd up to *public view.* I have somewhere read, that CATO, on seeing a young Nobleman coming out of the stews, uttered words to this purport, intent, or meaning:

When turgid lust distends the vital frame,
'Tis lawful to come here, and quench the flame.

F I N I S.

Lightning Source UK Ltd.
Milton Keynes UK
UKHW051106220722
406179UK00022B/764

9 781170 023624